Simple Low-Cost Games and Activities
for Sensorimotor Learning

by the same author

**Understanding Motor Skills in Children with Dyspraxia,
ADHD, Autism, and Other Learning Disabilities**
A Guide to Improving Coordination
Part of the *JKP Essentials* series
ISBN 978 1 84310 865 8
eISBN 978 1 84642 672 8

**Visual Perception Problems in Children with AD/
HD, Autism, and Other Learning Disabilities**
A Guide for Parents and Professionals
Part of the *JKP Essentials* series
ISBN 978 1 84310 826 9
eISBN 978 1 84642 505 9

How to Help a Clumsy Child
Strategies for Young Children with Developmental Motor Concerns
ISBN 978 1 84310 754 5
eISBN 978 1 84642 413 7

of related interest

**Playing, Laughing and Learning with
Children on the Autism Spectrum**
A Practical Resource of Play Ideas for Parents and Carers
2nd edition
Julia Moor
ISBN 978 1 84310 608 1
eISBN 978 1 84642 824 1

Motivate to Communicate!
300 Games and Activities for Your Child with Autism
Simone Griffin and Dianne Sandler
ISBN 978 1 84905 041 8
eISBN 978 0 85700 215 0

Can't Play Won't Play
Simply Sizzling Ideas to get the Ball Rolling for Children with Dyspraxia
Sharon Drew and Elizabeth Atter
ISBN 978 1 84310 601 2
eISBN 978 1 84642 758 9

**The Pocket Occupational Therapist for Families
of Children With Special Needs**
Cara Koscinski
ISBN 978 1 84905 932 9
eISBN 978 0 85700 721 6

Fun with Messy Play
Ideas and Activities for Children with Special Needs
Tracey Beckerleg
ISBN 978 1 84310 641 8
eISBN 978 1 84642 854 8

Simple Low-Cost Games and Activities for
SENSORIMOTOR
LEARNING

A Sourcebook of Ideas for Young Children Including Those with Autism, ADHD, Sensory Processing Disorder, and Other Learning Differences

Lisa A. Kurtz

Jessica Kingsley *Publishers*
London and Philadelphia

First published in 2014
by Jessica Kingsley Publishers
73 Collier Street
London N1 9BE, UK
and
400 Market Street, Suite 400
Philadelphia, PA 19106, USA

www.jkp.com

Library of Congress Cataloging in Publication Data
Kurtz, Lisa A.
  A sourcebook for sensorimotor learning : simple low-cost games and activities for young children
including those with autism, ADHD, sensory processing disorder, and other learning differences / Lisa A.
Kurtz.
    pages cm
  Includes bibliographical references and index.
  ISBN 978-1-84905-977-0 (alk. paper)
  1. Children with disabilities--Education. 2. Educational games. 3. Children with disabilities--Recreation.
  4. Perceptual-motor learning. 5. Sensory stimulation. I. Title.
  LC4026.K87 2014
  371.9--dc23
                                    2013035783

British Library Cataloguing in Publication Data
A CIP catalogue record for this book is available from the British Library

ISBN 978 1 84905 977 0
eISBN 978 0 85700 879 4

Printed and bound in Great Britain

CONTENTS

PREFACE

Since the early 1970s, I have enjoyed the privilege of working professionally with young children who have a wide range of abilities and challenges in home, school, community, and hospital settings. Although I have had exposure to just about any kind of disability a child might experience, I have always held a special interest for those children with developmental differences that impact learning, behavior, and social adjustment, such as autism, attention deficit disorders, sensory processing disorder, and specific learning disabilities. The activities described in this book are developed with those populations in mind, although most activities are also appropriate for children with typical development, and many can be easily adapted for children with other types of disabilities, including motor impairments (such as cerebral palsy), or sensory impairments (such as a vision or hearing impairment).

As an occupational therapist, I have been trained to carefully analyze the ways in which a child's unique abilities, interests, and environmental influences impact his behavior and development. With this information at hand, I am able to create an individualized intervention program that motivates a child to engage in meaningful activities that have been designed to overcome obstacles to his development, and to have lots of fun in the process. (For ease of reading, the gender pronoun has been alternated by chapter.) There is no specific formula for helping children to learn. Therapy looks different for each child, and often includes a wide range of components, such as specific exercises, seating and positioning devices, adapted tools and equipment, environmental modifications, parent and caregiver training and instruction, behavioral shaping strategies, and many more techniques than I could possibly describe in a brief description of my profession. The unifying theme in my therapy, however, is that whatever interventions I choose, they are *always* embedded in a playful activity that is enjoyable to the child as well as to myself. Without question, that is the best way to ensure motivation, enthusiasm, and effort on the part of the child. How lucky I am to get to play with children every single day that I go to work!

Parents, teachers, social workers, coaches, or other adults often approach me with questions about how they might help a child to follow through with their therapy goals. Of course, there are many *official* ways in which I am able to share my recommendations through parent conferences, in-service presentations, or informal hallway chats. Sadly, though, there never seems to be enough time for this kind of dialogue as the current economy drives greater and greater demands for cost-saving productivity and accountability. This book was developed as a resource to supplement the recommendations and guidelines that might occur as part of a therapy or special education process. Although my focus is on young children in preschool through elementary school years, some of the activities can be easily adapted to younger or older children.

Please understand that the ideas and suggestions included in this book are not intended to replace professional recommendations that may be specific to a child with a disability. Ultimately, a pediatrician or other appropriate health professional should be consulted to determine what types of activities are safe or unsafe for an individual child. Likewise, only a professional who knows and has worked with a child can determine whether certain activities are going to be therapeutically appropriate and beneficial.

If you are the parent of a child who has not been identified as having special needs, but are concerned about his development or behavior, start by discussing your concerns with the child's pediatrician. Be as specific as possible, and don't be afraid that the pediatrician will think you are being over reactive. In my experience, parents are notoriously excellent observers of their children, and all questions that parents might ask are good questions. Because of their many daily interactions with the child, parents have the opportunity to observe subtle differences in the way their child behaves that a doctor cannot possibly be aware of, given a short office visit every now and then. Pediatricians are well trained to perform a screening evaluation of a child's development. If a screening evaluation suggests delays, the pediatrician can then make referrals to the appropriate specialists for a more in-depth evaluation as indicated.

How therapies and special education services are funded and provided varies across countries. In the United States, children with disabilities are protected by the **Individuals with Disabilities Education Act**, initially passed in 1990 and revised in 2004 as the Individuals with Disabilities Education Improvement Act. This is federal legislation that governs how states and public agencies provide early intervention, special education, and related services to eligible children from birth through age 18 or 21 (depending upon the disability). Children from birth to age two may be eligible for early intervention services under Part C of this legislation, while children ages three to twenty-one may be eligible for special education and related services under Part B. For children who have not yet entered school, the pediatrician can inform parents how to go about requesting an evaluation through the appropriate state agency to determine what, if any, early intervention services the child may be eligible to receive. Once in school, the child may be eligible to receive special education and related services (which can include occupational or physical therapy) if they meet both federal and state standards for disability eligibility. Keep in mind, though, that not all children with disabilities are eligible to receive services through school. In order to qualify under the special education umbrella, the child must meet the criteria for having a disability, and must also be determined to require special education services in order to benefit from the educational program. In some cases, children with disabilities are able to learn adequately and are therefore not eligible for special education services, but require other supports and accommodations due to a disability or health-related problem. **Section 504 of the Rehabilitation Act of 1973** is federal civil rights legislation designed to prevent discrimination to persons with disabilities. In schools, this legislation may be appropriate for providing these children with the supports they need to access a public education. If your child is struggling in school and is not responding to efforts by the regular education staff to improve his performance, ask to sit down with a special education teacher to discuss the process for considering a referral for a special education evaluation, or for other options to receive school support.

In the United Kingdom (UK), students with disabilities or special learning needs are protected under the **Education Act of 1996**. Under this act, each of the countries in the United Kingdom has separate systems under separate governments for providing for students with **Special Education Needs**, or **SEN**. The services provided are widely variable throughout the UK, with a preference for maintaining students with disabilities in mainstream state schools, but with access to specialist schools in some circumstances. All publicly funded schools in the UK are required to maintain an SEN Coordinator position, and SEN services must follow an SEN Code of Practice which provides non-binding guidance on how educational supports are shaped and maintained.

Remember that publicly funded early intervention services and special education programs are not the only places to find help for a child with a disability. Parents need to understand that the mandate for public schools is to provide a free and appropriate *education* to all children, including those with disabilities or learning differences. The evaluations and services provided by schools are designed to support the *educational*, not medical, needs of the child. Many parents find the need to access services and supports in addition to those offered by the schools, especially when the diagnosis is serious, complicated, or requires medical supervision. When a significant disability exists, schools may not be equipped to offer specific recommendations about a child's prognosis, how to plan for the child's future, or when it may be appropriate to consider various medically based interventions. Many parents opt to obtain medical or therapy evaluations outside of the publicly funded sources, often accessing private insurance to pay for those services. Again, this is a good topic of discussion for the pediatrician.

My intention in writing this book was not to replace any recommendations made as part of an individualized therapy program developed for a specific child, but to help parents, teachers, and others involved in the lives of children with and without special needs to think creatively about how to play with the child in ways that support his development, using materials that are readily available in most households, or that can be purchased or homemade at a very low cost. In today's economy, there are few parents (or professionals, for that matter) who can afford to purchase very many of the commercially available toys and tools to support development. My own practice has always been to purchase a select few items that are harder to make or substitute, and then to make do with whatever I have on hand. I have been able to augment my therapy supplies substantially through creative stockpiling, for example:

- frequenting flea markets or yard sales, where sellers are often willing to give me an extra discount when they hear why I need a particular item

- making my own toys, or enlisting the help from willing volunteers when I lack the construction skill needed

- soliciting donations from parents whose children have outgrown the usefulness of their toys

- accessing online resources for children's crafts, worksheets and other activity suggestions.

Above all, this book is intended to open your eyes to the many possibilities for supporting a child's development through playful interactions. It doesn't need to take a lot of money, or even a very sophisticated knowledge of how children learn and grow. Almost any playful activity has the potential to teach. Let this book help to inspire you to think outside of the box when you have time to play with your children. As you experiment with the recommendations in this book, please strive to have as much fun, or maybe even more, than those special children in your lives!

Note: All emboldened terms in the main text are explained in the glossary at the end of the book.

Chapter 1

INTRODUCTION
The Importance of Play

Play is the universal passion of all children. All children play, although children (like their adult counterparts) have varying interests and abilities that impact their choice of playthings and play activities. Play is the means by which children explore, interact with, and master their environments, and is a critically important part of how children learn to develop physically, cognitively, and socially. Play allows children to find respite from the adult-directed structure of everyday life, and to feel successful while engaging in an activity that they truly enjoy. Child-initiated play is pursued voluntarily, is always self motivated, and is thoroughly engaging and enjoyable.

When an adult is hoping to entice a child to participate in play with the purpose of supporting development, the adult needs to ensure that the activity is enjoyable in the child's eyes, and also that she has sufficient skill to ensure success with the activity. One common-sense way to ensure that activities are enjoyable in the child's eyes is to design them around the child's unique interests. For example, a simple beanbag toss game can take many different forms:

- placing several cooking pots on the floor and throwing *ingredients* into the pot (for the food aficionado)

- lining up opened shoeboxes and pretending they are a train, then aiming for the engine or the caboose (for the child with a passion for trains)

- cutting out pictures of bugs and pasting them onto cardboard targets to *squash* (for the child who has more aggressive tendencies or who enjoys nature).

Children also need to feel in control in at least some aspects of the selected play activity in order to feel self directed. If you, as the adult, have suggested a game that is agreeable to the child, allow as much choice as feasible. For example, if the activity involves coloring, allow a choice of using crayons, markers, or chalk, and whether to color on white paper, recycled shopping bags, or construction paper. If the child tends to prefer more sedentary make-believe activities and you wish to introduce more physically challenging play, encourage the child to invite a favorite doll or stuffed animal to watch, or better yet, to join in on the game. Offer choices as to when to play a game (before lunch, or after lunch), in which environment (inside or outside), and with which participants (should a friend or sibling be invited to play?). Allow the child to let you know when she has had enough of a game. Children will let you know whether they are having fun or not. Avoid the temptation to push a child to continue playing if they are clearly tired, bored, or frustrated. You may succeed in getting the child to cooperate for your request, but learning requires effort on the part of the child, and if she is not having fun, it is unlikely that significant learning will occur.

It is also important to find as many opportunities as possible for providing immediate, positive reinforcement for a child's participation in a learning activity. Reinforcement can take many forms. Many children are reinforced through such simple measures as a high five, hug, or verbal compliment. Remember to reinforce the *effort* more than the actual end product. For example, let's say the child is working on a coloring page but really cannot do more than scribble. Try giving some concrete suggestion (for example, "Let's try holding the crayon *this* way," or "Let's see what happens when you slow down"), and then reinforce the child's response to your suggestion with statements like, "Look how well your fingers are holding that crayon!" or "Great job slowing down!" Many children also respond well to visual tools to reinforce their participation in learning activities. This can take many forms, and at school or in formal therapy programs may include a visual chart or schedule of activities the child is expected to do. As each activity is completed, the child might move a token to a "finished" column, or might receive a star or checkmark for each task completed. After a predetermined number of successes, the child then earns a small prize or "choice" time. An easy way to do this at home is to have a supply of index cards at hand, and tell the child that she must earn a certain number of stars, happy faces, or another symbol, in order to earn a preferred reward. Using a marker or self-inking stamper, you can give an immediate visual reward each time the child shows effort. This can be a very open-ended way of providing reinforcement, as the adult can control when a symbol has been earned. For example, the older child who generally shows good effort might earn a symbol for every completed activity. The younger or more easily frustrated child might earn more incremental rewards, such as one symbol for sitting at the table, another for choosing between markers or crayons, another for writing one letter in their name, and so forth. This can be a very promising way to gradually build tolerance for sustaining effort in non-preferred tasks!

When thinking about selecting which activities to choose, it is equally important to ensure that the child has the cognitive maturity and skill level to be successful. There are many factors that contribute to a child's rate and quality of development of sensorimotor skills. Genetic or inherited traits can impact overall strength, agility, and general talent for physical challenges. Culture and lifestyle preferences also play a role, as many children in today's society tend to be less interested in physical activities, and more and more entranced by the latest and most compelling technology developments. Developmental differences—common among children with autism, ADHD, and other learning differences—vary widely from child to child. Most children will acquire skills following fairly predictable stages known as **developmental milestones**. Because all children develop according to their own timeline, and children with disabilities may be delayed in acquiring certain milestones, it is important to select play activities that fit with the child's developmental level of skill, as opposed to their chronological age. If your child receives special education or therapy, you may be able to receive some guidance as to the child's developmental level by your child's teacher or therapist. Table 1.1 presents some of the more common developmental milestones that are expected of young children with typical development.

Table 1.1 Typical developmental milestones

Age	Fine motor	Gross motor	Speech/language	Cognitive/perceptual	Play
6 mos	Transfers toy from hand to hand Rakes at toy with all fingers	Plays with feet when lying on back Rolls in both directions Sits with hands propped forward Bounces on feet with hands held	Pays attention to music or singing Understands "hi" and "bye-bye" Imitates simple sounds like "ba-ba" or "wa-wa"	Shakes rattle on purpose Follows moving objects with eyes	No interest in peers Simple give-and-take play with family like tickling
9 mos	Grasps block with fingers Holds wrist in "bent back" position when holding objects	Head still lags when pulled to sit from lying on back Creeps or crawls Sits independently with hands free for play Pulls to stand at low table or bench	Stops activity when name is called Understands "no" Uses simple gestures, like pointing to desired object	Holds toys in each hand and brings together at midline	Plays "peek-a-boo" and "pat-a-cake"
12 mos	Stacks two blocks Grasps tiny object using pinch Holds crayon using fisted grasp Helps to turn pages in book	Stands alone without support Takes first steps holding hand	Responds to simple commands without gestures Knows one body part Beginning to use single words meaningfully	Imitates scribbling with crayon	Initiates familiar games, like "peek-a-boo" Simple imitation, like bringing empty spoon to mouth

cont.

Table 1.1 Typical developmental milestones *cont.*

Age	Fine motor	Gross motor	Speech/language	Cognitive/perceptual	Play
15 mos	Stacks three blocks Can place small pegs in holes Uses spoon to scoop with spilling	Walks independently Crawling is discarded, except on stairs Plays while squatting Gets to standing position without holding anything	Points to named object Points to several body parts	Enjoys fill-and-dump activities Scribbles with crayon without demonstration	Starting to show interest in other's play (watching) Likes books, points to or pats pictures
18 mos	Stacks four blocks Turns book pages alone, 2–3 at a time	Seats self in small chair Climbs stairs holding rail Seldom falls when walking	Refers to self by name Puts together two-word sentences	Inserts simple shapes into formboard	Talks to self, often using sing-song rhythm Experiments with movement
24 mos	Stacks seven blocks Strings small beads	Kicks a ball forward Jumps with both feet leaving floor Climbs stairs with two feet on each step	Produces 25–200 words Jargon has disappeared	Matches three colors Imitates simple strokes (circular scribble, vertical lines)	Enjoys listening to simple stories and nursery rhymes May hold out toys, but reluctant to share Stubborn (the "terrible twos")
30 mos	Stacks nine blocks Turns book pages singly Prefers one hand for crayon	Climbs stairs with one foot to each step Stands briefly on one foot Rides tricycle	Using more words to communicate ideas Fills in words or phrases to familiar stories	Imitates horizontal strokes Names own drawing, even if unrecognizable	Can play quietly for 10–15 minutes Still very possessive with toys

	Fine Motor	Gross Motor	Language	Cognitive	Social/Play
36 mos	Stacks 10 blocks Holds crayon with fingers like adult Cuts "fringe" with scissors	Runs on toes Runs, turning sharp corners without falling Can broad jump approximately 30cm (12") Can jump off low step	Vocabulary of about 1000 words 2 to 4 words in sentence Who, what, when, where, why questions Carries on purposeful conversation No longer repeats or echoes others	Imitates cross with crayon Names and sorts objects by color Counts three objects correctly	Parallel play, but interested in playing alongside others Imaginative play with dolls and stuffed animals More attentive to rules with fewer tantrums
4 yrs	Can place 10 raisins in small pill bottle within 20 seconds Shifts crayon up/down using fingers only to adjust Puts shoes/socks on correctly Washes and dries hands correctly Cuts a 2.5cm (1") line to within 0.16cm (¹⁄₁₆")	Hops on one foot Catches beanbag with the hands (not against the body) Can broad jump approximately 60cm (24") Throws ball overhead with control	Can recall four digits in correct sequence 4 to 5 word sentences Speech is 90% understandable Likes to tell stories to dolls or stuffed animals	Names some letters, numbers Copies square with crayon	Attends to play for 30 minutes Some turn taking and sharing with peers Likes to make things and is interested in product

cont.

Table 1.1 Typical developmental milestones *cont.*

Age	Fine motor	Gross motor	Speech/language	Cognitive/perceptual	Play
5 yrs	Can place 10 raisins in small pill bottle within 18 seconds Cuts out square within 0.6cm (¼") Dresses with minimal assistance Ties the half-knot on shoes	Runs through obstacle course avoiding obstacles Skips with alternating feet Stands on one foot for 10 seconds	Capable of long narratives Questions persistently	Counts 10 objects correctly Prints first name Draws recognizable person with body, stick limbs, facial features	Communicates with peers to organize activities Plays simple board games, but with little understanding of strategy Starting to understand that people have different thoughts and feelings about things
6 yrs	Can move coin from palm of hand to fingers to place in soda machine Uses knife/fork to cut Ties bow Writes name legibly and on line Able to carry fragile items safely	Performs one each of sit-up and knee push-up Rides two-wheeler	Likes silly stories and riddles 6 to 8 word sentences Starting to enjoy stories without illustrations	Copies triangle and crude diamond Prints all letters and numbers 1–9 without a model Performs simple addition and subtraction Discriminates left from right	Likes construction with attention to small details Cooperates with peers with more social give-and-take More rivalry in competitive games

It is also important to understand that children go through different stages of play interests and themes. For children aged 0–2 years, playtime tends to be very physical as children learn about themselves and the objects that occupy their world. Children at this age enjoy exploring their ever-expanding world by riding, pushing toys back and forth, pulling on things, placing objects in and out of containers, and in general, seeing how things work. From the age of two to four years, children like to learn by imitating what they see others doing, either by using actual objects or through make-believe. They are beginning to learn concepts such as shape, color, and number through play. They are also interested in putting objects, actions, and sounds together in simple constructions. This is the period when many children are introduced to simple art activities and learn to enjoy being creative. At this stage, children will play alongside each other, but do not typically engage reciprocally in play or willingly share toys. As children continue to mature at the ages of approximately four to seven, they become more interested in playing with other children, build more constructively, and engage in games that allow them to dramatize the things they are seeing out in the real world. This allows them to develop more mature social interactions with peers. As they play typical games like tag or board games, they learn many important social rules such as waiting for one's turn, following the rules, and learning how to win or lose graciously. Children at this age are often bossy or impatient with peers as they learn to negotiate the social expectations of play. Between 7 and 11 years of age, most children enjoy more complex games with rules, organized sports, and other activities that encourage a competitive spirit. This is also the time when many children become interested in specific hobbies such as crafts, collecting things, or joining clubs along with peers who have similar interests.

To begin using this book, start thinking about what skills you think your child needs to improve. Each section begins with a description of why that particular skill area is important to learning, and what might be the signs and symptoms that a child is struggling in that area. A therapist or teacher who works with your child may be helpful in steering you towards the most important areas to stress. Next, skim the book to find activities that you think your child might enjoy playing with you. Activities are grouped according to the primary skill area addressed, but most activities offer learning challenges in multiple areas. A quick reference guide for selecting activities is included in Appendix A (see p.122). For example, you might be focusing on improving balance, but want to find balance activities that also offer opportunities for working on **visual attention** and tracking, or perceptual skills. Appendix A offers an easy way for you to consider your options. Remember to use your own creativity to expand or modify the activities in any way that suits your child's interests, developmental level, or your available resources. Some of my most successful therapy sessions have occurred when I am challenged to think on the spot and just have fun!

Please remember that this book is designed as a general guide and not as a formal occupational therapy program for your child. I have attempted to provide a general overview of some of the most important concepts involved in sensorimotor learning, but I wanted to focus more on the creative use of activities than on the rationale behind sensorimotor learning approaches. The resource section, located in Appendix C, offers a comprehensive list of books and other resources for the reader who wishes to delve deeper into understanding the nature of sensorimotor learning differences in children with disabilities. Remember, too, that some of the activities described may not be appropriate for every child. For example, children with certain medical problems may be limited in the amount of physical activity they can safely undergo, and some parents will want to avoid activities that might expose their child to latex, dyes, or other materials that might trigger sensitivities. Check with your child's pediatrician or therapist if you have any concerns. Some activities require materials that could be unsafe for certain children, for example because they involve small parts that could become a choking hazard, or because they use materials that could cause allergic reactions to sensitive children. Always use common sense and closely supervise any activity that could potentially cause risk to a young child. I've learned to expect the unexpected when I am working with children, and am extra careful especially with gross motor activities, or when working with materials that might be thrown, or that might find their way into a child's mouth!

One final note—think carefully about how you engage the child in conversation about why you are asking her to participate in these activities. Many very young children are happy to play just for the sake of having fun, but others have an emerging understanding of their differences, or require more encouragement to put effort into tasks that are challenging. This is the perfect opportunity to talk about how every person has unique differences, and to introduce some basic information about the child's disability. Many children actually feel empowered when they learn that there is a reason why they have a hard time doing certain things that other children can do easily. Playing therapeutically with a child provides the perfect opportunity to offer your observations as to what things are hard or easy for a particular child, to offer positive feedback for effort (not just success) with the activities, and to engage in collaborative problem-solving for making things easier. I use my sessions with children to offer simple explanations about why various games or activities are important for helping them in ways that are meaningful to them. Some examples of simple explanations I might use include:

- "When we play 'treasure hunt' it helps your eyes to get better at noticing small details. That should make it much easier for you at school when you are learning how to read."

- "I notice that you are getting stronger every time that we practice these balancing games. That's great, because children who have strong bodies find it easier to sit still and pay attention to learning when they are at school."

- "Look how strong your fingers are getting! I'll bet that means your hand won't get so tired when you have to write a lot of words!"

- "I notice that your body looks calmer when we play this game."

- "Let's find out if it's easier for you to cut on the line when you hold your scissors like this."

Appendix C also includes a list of recommended child-friendly storybooks that can be used to help children develop a beginning understanding of disabilities. Many of these are especially useful in helping friends or siblings understand why some children learn or behave differently, and how they can be of help.

Chapter 2

PROMOTING GROSS MOTOR SKILLS

RELATIONSHIP TO LEARNING

Gross motor skills refer to those body movements that involve large muscle groups and total body movements. Examples of these include crawling, walking, running, balancing, throwing and catching a ball, or climbing on playground equipment. Newborn infants have very little voluntary control over their gross motor movements, but quickly start to develop control of the head and neck muscles within the first few weeks of life. As the young child grows and matures, most typical young children exhibit high levels of energy as they are intuitively driven to explore their environment in a very active manner. Just think of how much energy most toddlers exhibit when they play! This is nature's way of making sure that children regularly exercise their muscles in order to develop control of their posture, balance, strength, and coordination.

Physical exploration of the environment also results in exposure to many different perceptual experiences through all of the body senses. These include the familiar sensations of vision, touch, hearing, taste and smell, but also certain sensations specific to gross motor control, including **vestibular** awareness (sense of gravity and motion originating from receptors in the inner ear), and **proprioceptive** awareness (sense of body motion and position originating from receptors in the joints and muscles). As the child experiences sensory input during movement activities, the brain processes that information, decides how the body should respond, and then sends signals to the appropriate muscles so the body can take action. In this way, the sensory feedback that occurs during gross motor activities is an important factor in the motor learning process. Gross motor skills require considerable practice and repetition in order to develop. Children who do not enjoy physical challenges, or who have sensory processing differences that result in confusing or unpleasant sensory experiences during movement, may be less willing than other children to independently explore their environment, and consequently receive less practice in developing their motor skills.

Although gross motor skills are most rapidly developed during the first two years of life, they continue to improve and become increasingly automatic well into the adult years. Gross motor skills are considered the foundation for many higher-level learning and behavioral skills. For example, the ability to maintain an upright posture during desk work at school is needed in order to stay alert and pay attention, to provide a stable base of support so that the hands can engage in controlled fine motor activities, and for keeping the head in a steady position so that the eyes can move and track smoothly without head movement during reading or other activities requiring visual attention.

STRENGTH AND ENDURANCE

Strength and endurance are critical to the development of gross motor skills. **Strength** is defined as the amount of force produced during a muscle contraction. **Endurance** is the ability to sustain physical effort over time. Most healthy and active children will naturally gain in their overall strength and endurance as they mature, but several common factors can contribute to decreased strength and endurance. **Muscle tone** refers to the length of muscles at rest, before a contraction, and is very variable among individuals. Children with significant neurological disabilities, such as cerebral palsy or traumatic brain injury, often experience high muscle tone, or **hypertonia**. Hypertonic muscles are shorter than average when at rest, which makes joints seem rigid and inflexible. In contrast, many children with milder learning differences such as autism, attention deficit disorders, or learning disabilities have low muscle tone, or **hypotonia**. Hypotonic muscles are longer than average when at rest, which causes increased flexibility and decreased stability of joints. Some people use the term **double-jointedness** to describe this condition. Children with hypotonia tend to have decreased strength, endurance, and **postural stability**. Some people believe that they may also experience less sensory feedback from movement experiences, making it harder for them to learn new or unfamiliar motor skills. Children who prefer a more sedentary lifestyle are also at risk of developing decreased strength and endurance because they spend less time in active play. The development of strength and endurance is critically important for maintaining an overall healthy lifestyle, for preventing obesity and related health concerns, and for helping to prevent childhood injuries.

BODY AWARENESS

Body awareness, also called proprioception, is the unconscious sense of body position and movement that comes from sensory receptors located in the joints and muscles of the body. This is the sense that allows us to accurately perform familiar movements such as wiping our nose or buttoning a shirt even if our eyes are closed. It allows us to make automatic, continual, unconscious adjustments to our body positions according to the particular demands of a task. For example, when a child attempts to catch a ball, he must reach in the direction of the ball, position the hands appropriately, maintain balance, and judge both the speed and direction of the ball as a moving target. The eyes inform the child whether he is likely to be successful, so body movements can be adjusted accordingly. In the process of catching a ball, the child gives very little conscious thought as to how the body feels when performing these adjustments. Children with poor body awareness need to pay conscious attention to movements that should otherwise occur automatically. For example, if asked to imitate arm and hand movements rapidly, the child with poor body awareness may have to look back and forth at the adult's arm, then his own arm, to make sure the movement is performed correctly. In general, children with decreased body awareness lack fluency and speed in performing motor movements that should be automatic. They often appear clumsy or disorganized when compared to other children their age.

MOTOR PLANNING

Motor planning is the ability to conceptualize, plan, and execute non-automatic movements and motor sequences. It is sometimes referred to as **praxis**, and children who have decreased skill in this area are considered **dyspraxic**. In normal motor planning, the child must possess a clear mental picture of what should occur, precise vestibular and proprioceptive feedback during movement, and the ability to make rapid, automatic adjustments to movement in time and space. Children with motor planning difficulties typically appear awkward when moving, have difficulty learning motor skills at a rate comparable to that of their peers, and have difficulty generalizing a learned motor skill to a new situation. For example, children typically first learn to tie a bow when they are learning to tie their shoelaces. Once learned, most children can easily transfer this skill to tying a bow on a package, or a ribbon in their hair, but children with motor planning difficulties struggle with the transfer of this skill to new or unfamiliar situations. Often, children with motor planning difficulties are easily frustrated and avoid challenging motor activities, and tend to be disorganized in their use of time and materials. Motor planning is not the same thing as motor coordination. A child with motor planning difficulties may, in fact, have very good coordination for challenging motor skills once those skills have been learned and committed to memory.

BALANCE

Balance refers to the ability to maintain a stable body position, and comes in two types. **Static balance** is the ability to maintain a position while the body is stationary, such as when standing on one foot. **Dynamic balance** is the ability to maintain position and manage postural changes while the body is moving, such as when running on an uneven surface. Balance requires the integration of multiple sensory inputs. Vestibular sensory input from the inner ear informs the brain about the effects of motion and gravity on postural control. Proprioceptive sensory input from the joints and muscles informs the brain about where the body is in relation to the world. Visual sensory input aids in estimating how close or far away an object is from our body (called **depth perception**), and in its orientation in relation to our body (called **spatial awareness**). Children with learning differences may have problems with one or more of these sensory processing skills affecting balance.

BILATERAL INTEGRATION

Bilateral integration refers to the ability of the two sides of the body to cooperate with each other during execution of motor activities. It develops gradually over time, leads to the development of a dominant hand for performing skilled motor activities, is a factor in automaticity of motor planning, and contributes to the cognitive awareness of certain spatial concepts, such as left and right orientation.

Most children begin to show a preference for using one hand at about two and a half years of age, and by the start of kindergarten will consistently use the dominant hand when manipulating crayons, pencils, or scissors. Children who do not have a clear hand preference by the time they enter school are at a disadvantage because a large portion of the school day is spent in performing fine motor activities. Certain fine motor activities are performed slightly differently when using the right versus the left hand. For example, writing paper is positioned differently for right and left-handed children, so that left-handed children can see what they write as they place letters from left to right across the page. Children who switch hands during writing can become confused about how to hold and position the pencil and paper, so these movements do not become automatic and habitual. Switching hands when manipulating objects that require less skill, such as blocks or beads, is not necessarily considered to be a problem, and may continue throughout childhood. Some people believe that a tendency to switch hands and to fail to develop a dominant side may be related to a problem with vestibular processing. Often, children switch hands because they are uncomfortable reaching across the midline of their body, so they choose to use the hand that is closest to the object being manipulated. Other children switch hands because of decreased hand strength. As they use one hand and start to become fatigued, they switch to the other hand to allow their tired hand to rest.

Common signs of difficulty with gross motor skills include:

- slow to achieve gross motor milestones (see Table 1.1)

- trips or falls more frequently than other children

- avoids playground, sports or other physically challenging activities

- reacts with strong emotion (positive or negative) to common movement experiences, such as swings or riding an elevator

- appears stiff or clumsy when walking or running

- frequently bumps into furniture or other people

- manipulates objects roughly or with too much force, often dropping or breaking items

- gets tired more easily than other children

- has a difficult time learning new skills, such as riding a bike or tying shoes

- fails to show a clear hand preference by age five

- has difficulty using the two sides of the body together (for example, skipping, performing jumping jacks, or holding paper down during drawing or coloring).

GROSS MOTOR ACTIVITIES

◼ 1 WHEELBARROW WALK

Primary learning focus

- Strength, body awareness, motor planning, bilateral integration.
- Tends to be a calming and organizing activity.

Materials needed

- None.

Description

The child assumes a crawling position on the floor with arms out straight and the palms of the hand flat on the floor. The adult then grasps the child by the ankles (or the knees for a child with poorer strength and control) and lifts so that the child can walk on his arms assisted by the adult. Encourage the child to keep his back and neck straight. This activity generates a lot of heavy work and proprioceptive input, and can be used for transitions from one room to another, or can be turned into a game, such as walking around obstacles.

Variations

- Spread beanbags or wads of newspaper around the room for the child to pick up with one hand and throw at a target. This requires shifting weight to one side in order to throw, which encourages more strength, bilateral integration, and eye-hand coordination.

- Build in practice for cognitive skills by asking the child to count how many steps they can take without falling, or by instructing them to walk around a room and see how many things they can find that are red, or square, or soft.

- Encourage memory skills by asking the child to recall a series of targets to walk towards (for example, "Let's take three steps towards the couch, then five steps towards the door").

- Use wheelbarrow walking as a calming transition activity, for example, walking to the bedroom for a nap, or to the closet to get outerwear for a trip outdoors.

2 ANGELS IN THE SNOW

Primary learning focus

- Body awareness, motor planning, bilateral integration.

Materials needed

- None.

Description

The child lies on his back on the rug or floor. The adult asks the child to make "angels" by opening and closing arms and legs in a synchronized manner. Try different patterns of movement, such as moving only the arms or legs, moving only the arm and leg on the right side, moving only the left arm and right leg, or moving everything except the left leg.

Variations

- Tie red ribbons on the right arm and leg ("red" is for "right") if the child is confused about these terms.

- Ask the child to close his eyes, then gently touch the parts to be moved to enhance body awareness.

- Ask the child to recall a two-step pattern, for example move only the arms five times, then only the legs five times, and continue the sequence.

- Tie a jingle bell around the limbs that should not move—if a bell rings, the child knows he has made a mistake.

3 MAGIC CARPET

Primary learning focus

- Strength, balance, motor planning, bilateral integration.
- Tends to be a calming activity.

Materials needed

- Carpet sample square, fuzzy side up.
- A slippery floor, such as tile or linoleum.

Description

The child assumes different postures on the magic carpet (sitting, kneeling, tummy lying, back lying) and propels himself (forwards or backwards) using arms and legs. Try to encourage the child to be as creative as possible in trying different ways to move the magic carpet.

Variations

- Create a simple obstacle course using pillows or cardboard boxes, and draw a "map" of the course to show where to go.
- Hide a specified number of small toys (for example, 10 toy cars, or 25 Lego pieces) for the child to find and place on the carpet; when all have been found and counted, the child gets to play with them.
- Let the child sit cross legged on the carpet, holding a rope or hula hoop while an adult pulls the child around a room.
- Substitute two lids from shoeboxes, have the child step into the lids and practice "skating" around the room.

■ 4 BALANCE BEAM

Primary learning focus

- Balance, body awareness, motor planning, strength.

Materials needed

- An area of grass or rug that is soft and safe to fall on (move potential dangerous obstacles away from the balance beam).
- Improvised balance beam—consider a 5cm × 10cm (2" × 4") wooden beam, garden hose, or large wooden building blocks placed end on end.

Description

Ask the child to practice walking the beam using a variety of approaches, including forward, backwards, sideways, heel-to-toe. Be sure that the child is barefoot, or wearing sensible shoes for this activity (for example, no flip-flops or Crocs). If the child feels very insecure, providing gentle support at the hips is better than holding the child's hand, since that might cause the child to lean towards the adult's hand, losing his balance.

Variations

- If the child is fearful of the balance beam, start by using a non-raised line made of masking tape, or use chalk to draw a line on the sidewalk.

- Place small objects on either side of the beam, so the child must squat to pick them up without falling; or give the child a handful of small objects like buttons or beads, place a row of empty soda bottles next to the beam, and have him bend to put one object in each bottle (increase the challenge by placing the objects in the child's dominant hand, and the bottles on the opposite side of the beam, so he must cross the midline to perform the task).

- Walk the beam while balancing something on the head.

- Walk the beam while holding a spoon in each hand, and balancing a ball or plastic Easter egg in each spoon.

- With very close adult supervision, try walking the beam with eyes closed.

■ 5 MAKING STATUES

Primary learning focus

- Trunk strength, balance, body awareness.

Materials needed

- None.

Description

Ask the child to assume various positions, for example on hands and knees with one hand on a hip, or standing while bracing hands against knees. Challenge the child to be "stiff like a statue—don't let me knock you down." Next, apply firm but gentle pressure to hips, shoulder, etc. in a gentle effort to break the pose. This requires the child to contract and stabilize the weight-bearing muscles in order to maintain balance.

Variations

- Have the child watch you as you assume a posture, then try to imitate the posture, requiring motor planning skills.

- Try this activity with eyes closed to increase body awareness.

▪ 6 T-STOOL GAMES (SEE APPENDIX B FOR DIRECTIONS)

Primary learning focus

- Balance, body awareness, bilateral integration, eye-hand co-ordination.

Materials needed

- Homemade T-stool.
- Various items to roll, throw, catch (beanbags, koosh balls, marbles to put in empty coffee can with hole in plastic top).

Description

A T-stool (one-legged stool) is a versatile piece of equipment that challenges a child to balance while sitting with an unstable base of support. T-stools can be used at a desk or table during any fine motor activity, but there are also many simple games that can take place while sitting on the stool. Teach the child to place feet well in front of the body, and to lean slightly forward to maintain a center of gravity. Once balanced on the stool, try engaging the child in various action songs (like itsy-bitsy spider, or head-shoulder-knees and toes) while balancing on the stool. Or play simple games of catch with a soft ball.

Variations

- Using an empty coffee can with a hole punched in the plastic lid, roll marbles towards the child, who must catch them and push them through the hole.
- Aim marbles or balls purposely in a direction that requires the child to cross his midline in order to catch.
- For the child who has difficulty with eye-hand coordination, use bubbles or balloons to hit, as these items move more slowly than heavier objects.

▪ 7 OBSTACLE COURSE

Primary learning focus

- Strength, motor planning, balance, sequential memory, spatial awareness.

Materials needed

- An assortment of objects to move in, under, on, or around, such as non-fragile pieces of furniture, large pillows, or cardboard boxes.

Description

Set up an obstacle course using whatever materials are at hand, but be sure to vary the challenges by including things to go over, under, or around. Ask the child to maneuver the obstacle course using different modes of locomotion, and following a sequence of directions (for example, "crawl under the table, then hop around the sofa two times, then crab-walk to the big cushion and let yourself crash").

Variations

- Try it with eyes closed, making sure the child will be safe, to increase body awareness.

- Use one mode of locomotion (for example, walking or crawling) but increase the number of steps the child needs to recall.

- Draw a simple picture of the obstacle course, and then place it in a clear plastic sheet protector. Using a wipe-off marker or crayon, draw a simple "map" for the child to follow. Alternatively, have the child "read" the map out loud, while you maneuver the obstacle course — this requires the child to practice using the vocabulary that describes spatial concepts.

■ 8 LOG ROLL

Primary learning focus

- Motor planning, bilateral coordination.
- Tends to be an energizing activity.

Materials needed

- Beanbags, koosh ball, or small stuffed animals.

Description

Teach the child to lie down on a soft surface and practice rolling in a perfectly straight line. This is harder than it looks, and requires considerable motor planning. If needed, use something to use as a visual guide for rolling straight (for example, rolling on a large foam mat, or creating boundaries by using masking tape or cushions). Have the child place a beanbag or other small, soft object in a particular location on their body (for example, between the wrists with hands held above head, between the knees, under the chin, or in the armpit) and then roll to a specified location without dropping the beanbag.

Variations

- Try it with eyes closed to increase body awareness.
- Try rolling faster or slower to see what difference it makes in rolling straight.
- Have the child lie down at one end of a large sheet or blanket, hold onto the edge, and roll so that he gets wrapped up in the blanket to make a "hot dog".

◾ 9 MAKE-A-KITE

Primary learning focus

- Strength, motor planning, bilateral integration.
- Tends to be an energizing activity.

Materials needed

- Plastic grocery bag without holes.
- String.
- Ribbons, crepe paper strips.

Description

Tie the two handles of the bag together at the very top, so that the bag looks like it has two "U's" at the top. Tape or staple ribbons or strips of paper at the bottom of the bag (to make streamers) and decorate the bag using permanent markers if desired. Tie a length of string to the U-shaped handles. Encourage the child to hold the string and run as fast as he can, so that wind will enter the kite to help keep it flying.

Variations

- Try making two kites, one for each hand.
- Have the child run to different targets according to a sequence (for example, "run to the back door, then to the red bush, then to the swings") to encourage memory and sequencing skills.
- Jump off a step or low obstacle, pretending that the bag is a parachute.

▉ 10 BELLY TIME

Primary learning focus

- Core trunk strength, body awareness, motor planning.
- Tends to be a calming activity.

Materials needed

- Miscellaneous fine motor games (coloring sheets, dot-to-dot, mazes, building blocks, etc.).
- Simple board games, such as Candyland or Chutes and Ladders.
- Book to read or pictures to look at.
- i-pad games.

Description

Spending time while lying on one's belly and propping upper body weight on the elbows helps to build strength in the shoulder, trunk, and neck muscles, and also provides powerful proprioceptive input. Encourage the child to play various games while in this position, aiming to increase the amount of time he can tolerate the position.

Variations

- Incorporate belly time as part of an obstacle course.
- Adapt a favorite board game by creating a set on index cards with the name of a physical exercise or activity written on each card (for example, "hop five times on each foot," or "tightrope walk to the sink and back"). Then, choose a color for each player. When a player lands on his selected color, he must take a card from the top of the pile and perform that activity a specified number of times. For children who do not enjoy physical activities, include some cards with fun consequences, like "Get a hug from Mom," or "Give me a high five" or "Eat an M&M of the specified color."
- If needed, you can roll up a towel or small blanket to place under the child's chest, making it a little easier to prop on the arms.
- Some children have an easier time keeping their head up if the activity is placed on a slanted surface, for example a large three-ring binder.

11 THE SUPERMARKET GAME

Primary learning focus

- Strength, proprioceptive input, bilateral integration.
- Tends to be a calming activity.

Materials needed

- Sturdy plastic laundry basket.
- An assortment of objects to go "shopping" for, preferably including some heavier items like telephone books, canned goods, boxes of rice, etc.

Description

Place items around the room or house, and then ask the child to push the laundry basket (the "shopping cart") to collect items. Older children can read an actual shopping list; younger children can get one item at a time, and then check in with the adult to find out what is next on the list. Pushing the heavy cart is a great heavy work activity that builds strength and proprioceptive awareness.

Variations

- Count how many items are in the basket, guessing what letter each item begins with, or identifying the first letter sound for each item (for example, "T" for telephone book, "C" for can, etc.).
- Play this game outdoors, substituting a wagon or other wheeled toy for collecting items.
- Have the child search for items to collect by category, for example, "find something you cannot eat," "find something brown," "find a vegetable," etc.

12 BALLOON TWISTER

Primary learning focus

- Balance, motor planning.

Materials needed

- Balloon.

Description

Have the child practice tapping a balloon to see how long he can keep it in the air. Count the number of taps to practice counting (or count by two's, or recite the alphabet to see how far he can go).

Variations

- Try batting the balloon with different body parts (elbow, knee, head), or according to a sequence or pattern (right knee, left knee).

- Tie different color ribbons on the right and left wrist, if the child is too young to understand the concepts "right" and "left".

- Try it while standing on a slightly unstable surface, such as a sofa cushion, to improve balance.

- Play "pass" with a partner, and have each partner call out what body part is next.

▓ 13 EGG RACES

Primary learning focus

- Balance, body awareness, motor planning.

Materials needed

- Plastic Easter eggs.

- Spoons, scoops, or measuring cups.

- Box, basket, or large unbreakable mixing bowl.

- Miscellaneous materials for filling eggs, for example, sand, rice, dry beans.

- Tape.

Description

Establish a starting point and an ending point for a race, with the box or bowl at the end of the race. Give the child a spoon to pick up eggs and carry to the finish line without dropping. Filling the eggs with something makes them heavier and easier to balance on the spoon—just be sure to tape them closed so that they will not open accidentally and make a mess! This is a great game to play alone (try timing the child's speed) or with one or more partners.

Variations

- Place a balance beam, pillows, or rope to balance on when carrying eggs to the finish line.

- Try carrying one egg in each hand.

- Have the child balance a beanbag or small stuffed animal on his or head and try to get to the finish line without dropping either the egg or the beanbag.

- Discard the spoon, and have the child crawl to the finish line pushing the egg with his nose, or crab walk and push the egg with a foot.

- Have two children stand side by side holding hands, with each partner holding one spoon in their free hand—the partners must work together to reach the finish line without dropping an egg.

14 MONKEY TOES

Primary learning focus

- Balance, motor planning, crossing the midline.

Materials needed

- Unbreakable bowl, bucket, or tote bag.
- Cotton balls, pompoms, or other small, soft objects.

Description

Scatter the cotton balls or other objects around a small area, and then have the child remove shoes and socks and collect the objects to place in the container using only his feet. If a cotton ball is too far away, have the child retrieve it and then hop on one foot to get to the container.

Variations

- Use different size or color pompoms, and have the child collect items according to size, color, or a pattern.

- Have the child sit on his bottom, and use two feet together to pick up objects.

- Have the child trap a beanbag between both feet, then jump on two feet to get to the container without losing the beanbag.

- Challenge balance skills by doing this activity with arms held over the head, hands in pockets or behind the back, or on a slightly unstable surface (for example, sofa cushion or air mattress).

15 CRAB-WALK SOCCER

Primary learning focus

- Strength, balance, motor planning.

Materials needed

- Beach ball or playground ball.
- Something to use as a goal (for example, laundry basket or large cardboard box placed on one side).

Description

Have the child assume a crab-walk position (on hands and legs with belly facing the ceiling, holding bottom off the floor), while he attempts to kick the ball into the goal, or defends the goal while you try to get the ball into the goal. This takes a great deal of heavy work involving the core trunk muscles, and provides a tremendous amount of proprioceptive and vestibular input.

Variations

- Play with a partner, each defending his own goal.
- Turn it into a relay, where the child picks up one ball, balances it on his belly while crab-walking to the goal, then sits down to throw the ball into the goal.
- Try playing soccer using different animal walks, such as "duck walking" (child squats and holds ankles, then tries to kick the ball with feet into the goal), or "elephant walking" (child bends over and holds hands together like an elephant's "trunk," using the trunk to maneuver the ball into the goal).

16 YOGA BALLS

Primary learning focus

- Balance, strength, motor planning.
- Tends to be a calming activity.

Materials needed

- Inflatable yoga ball (these can be found inexpensively at discount stores, but I have found them at yard sales costing almost nothing).
- A soft, safe surface with no nearby obstacles (outdoors on the lawn, or indoors on a mat or soft rug, well away from furniture).

Description

The child sits on the ball with an adult holding the child's hips. Tilt the ball in various directions, asking the child to maintain his balance. Experiment with different positions, such as lying back on the ball then trying to sit up, or belly lying over the ball and bearing weight on the arms.

Variations

- Place beanbags or other objects for the child to pick up and throw at a target or container without losing balance.

- Have the child hold one side of a hula hoop while you hold the other side, and let the child experiment with controlling his balance on the ball.

- Sit on the ball while sitting at a desk or table and playing a game.

- Use the ball to play pass, or for practicing how to dribble—the large size and weight of the ball makes it move more slowly than other balls, so it is easier to control.

- Sit on the ball and bounce up and down to the rhythm of favorite music—this is very calming for some children.

17 THE POPCORN GAME

Primary learning focus

- Strength, bilateral integration.
- Tends to be an energizing activity.

Materials needed

- Bed sheet or blanket (smaller size works better).
- Balloons, small stuffed animals, lightweight balls or other objects to serve as the "popcorn."

Description

Two people stand at each side of the sheet holding on to the edge (or better yet, this game is even more fun with more people holding onto different sides of the sheet). Place the soft objects in the center of the sheet, then shake up and down as hard as you can until all of the objects have been "popped" and have spilled from the sheet.

Variations

- Practice counting or saying the alphabet with each shake.

- Use a marker to draw shapes, numbers, or letters on balloons, or use pieces of paper with symbols that have been wadded into balls—see which one is the first to leave the sheet and which is the last.

- Try it with eyes closed to see if the child can tell by feel when everything has left the sheet.

■ 18 ZOOM TUBE (SEE APPENDIX B FOR DIRECTIONS)

Primary learning focus

- Strength, bilateral integration, motor planning.

Materials needed

- Homemade zoom tube.

Description

A zoom tube is a cardboard tube, outfitted with two long strings inserted through the middle, and loops tied at each end of the two strings to form "handles." The child holds two handles, one in each hand, with a partner holding the other two handles. Each partner stands just far enough away that the two strings are kept taut (this is really hard for young children, and requires considerable body awareness and motor planning). One partner opens arms wide while the other partner simultaneously brings arms together, causing the zoom tube to fly towards the partner whose arms are held together. It will require a good deal of shoulder and arm strength, as well as teamwork, to keep the zoom tube moving back and forth.

Variations

- Try zooming with arms held overhead, or facing away from the partner with arms held behind the back.

- Zoom to the beat of music, while counting or skip counting, or for the older child, while spelling out words.

- Vary the length of the strings—longer strings require more control than shorter ones.

■ 19 SCOOPING CUPS (SEE APPENDIX B FOR DIRECTIONS)

Primary learning focus

- Strength, balance, motor planning, bilateral integration.

Materials needed

- Homemade scooping cups.
- Beanbag, koosh ball, or wadded tissue paper ball.

Description

Scooping cups are a little bit like jai-alai, but the scoops are much bigger and easier for children to use. Teach the child to hold one scoop with the opening facing towards the ceiling. Place a beanbag or other soft projectile in the cup, and teach the child to toss it in the air and catch it again with the scoop. Once the child has learned to be successful with one scoop, provide another scoop for the other hand and practice tossing with one hand and catching with the other.

Variations

- Use scoops to play catch with a partner, each holding one scoop.
- Use two scoops to catch according to a pattern, for example, left, left, right.
- Substitute large plastic drinking cups and ping-pong balls; place a ball into one cup, tip it over to bounce on the floor or table, and catch it with the other cup.
- Play catch while sitting on a yoga ball or T-stool, or while standing in a confined space, such as on a sofa cushion.

■ 20 THE DRESS-UP RACE

Primary learning focus

- Strength, motor planning, body awareness, fine motor dexterity.

Materials needed

- Assorted clothes, preferably a little too large for the child (use a parent or sibling's clothes, or collect from a thrift shop).
- Something to mark the start and end of the race.
- Index cards and marker.
- Egg timer or watch.

Description

Place clothes at one end of the race, and position the child (or children) at the start. Each child should have an index card with his name on. When the adult says, "go," the child must run to the clothes and don one item, then return to the start. If the piece of clothing is on correctly, the child gets a star or happy face on his card, and runs to don another piece of clothing. This game can be played solo (use the timer or watch to see how long it takes to don a designated number of items), or as a race with another player (see who correctly dons all items first).

Variations

- For the child who is having trouble with a particular skill, such as managing zippers or buttons, have several items that challenge only that skill—the child must don the item, then take it off before donning the next item.

- To increase the motor planning challenge, try donning clothing (omitting the fasteners) while wearing mittens.

- Increase the listening challenge by providing a verbal clue indicating the next clothing item ("Put on something striped" or "Put on something for a rainy day").

▉ 21 SHADOW MAKER

Primary learning focus

- Body awareness, motor planning, bilateral integration.
- Tends to be a calming activity.

Materials needed

- Empty wall.
- Darkened room with a strong lamp or lantern.

Description

Have the child stand in front of the adult, facing the wall, with the light shining behind both so that their shadows are projected against the wall. Instruct the child to keep his shadow "inside" of the adult's shadow. The adult assumes various body postures, while the child tries to imitate the posture (without looking at the adult). If done correctly, the child's shadow will remain invisible inside of the larger adult's shadow.

Variations

- Practice animal walks to see what their shadows look like.
- Practice hand shadows patterns.
- Let the adult sit next to the child and use his finger to make a shape or a letter of the alphabet, while the child tries to imitate.

- Learn the sign language alphabet—great for fine motor planning—and practice these during shadow play.

22 CHARADES

Primary learning focus

- Motor planning, body awareness, bilateral integration.

Materials needed

- Index cards, old magazines.
- Egg timer.

Description

Search through magazines to find pictures of things that can fit different categories, such as "animals," "sports," or "things that parents do," being careful to choose categories that will require moving the whole body to act out the picture. Glue the pictures onto one side of each card, and mark the other side to indicate the category (for example, red = animal, blue = sports). The child takes turns selecting a card, looking at the picture, and then acting it out for another player (or players) to guess before the timer runs out. Set the timer for about 15 seconds per turn, or longer for a child who really struggles with this activity.

Variations

- Play the game silently, without making any noises, to increase the challenge.
- For older children, choose categories that require more abstract concepts, for example preparing different foods, or acting out a particular TV program or star.

23 RHYTHM STICKS

Primary learning focus

- Bilateral integration, motor planning.

Materials needed

- Sticks for tapping, two per child (you can use paper towel tubes, drumsticks, unsharpened pencils, knitting needles—whatever you have).

Description

Start by using rhythm sticks to keep time to familiar tunes. Once this is mastered, try teaching the child to imitate different patterns that the adult demonstrates (for example, a two-step pattern would be right, left, right, left, while a more difficult pattern might be right, right, both, left, left, both). Many children can do this while facing the adult who demonstrates the pattern, but others find it easier if the adult sits behind them. If the child is getting confused about which stick to use, provide a visual cue by having both the adult and the child wear different colored ribbons on each wrist (for example, red for right wrist and blue for left wrist), or by holding different colored sticks in each hand.

Variations

- Vary the qualities of the pattern by hitting harder or softer, faster or slower.

- Instead of demonstrating a pattern, use verbal directions to indicate the pattern (for example, tap two times with the left stick, then one time with the right stick).

- Tie ribbons or strips of crepe paper to the end of the sticks, and have the child follow motions with the sticks without an auditory cue.

- Use two sticks that produce different sounds when tapping the floor or table—the child closes his eyes to hear the pattern then attempts to copy the pattern.

■ 24 I WENT TO THE GYM…

Primary learning focus

- Strength, body awareness, motor planning, memory.
- Tends to be a calming activity.

Materials needed

- Nothing—just a safe area for exercising.

Description

This is a variation of the classic memory game "I went on a shopping trip and bought a… ," where each player must add an item until someone forgets the correct order of the shopping list. In this variation, players say, "I went to the gym and I did… " adding exercises (for example, hopping, skipping, jumping jacks, etc.). The child acts out the exercises in the sequence, instead of using words. This is a good way to build strength and endurance while burning off excess energy!

Variations
Choose other themes that can be acted out, for example "I went to the zoo and I saw a monkey eating a banana… ," or "I went to school and I read a book and colored a picture…" while acting out each motion.

OTHER IDEAS FOR SUPPORTING GROSS MOTOR DEVELOPMENT

- Use playground equipment for climbing, swinging, sliding.
- Play twister.
- Use tin can stilts.
- Practice animal walks.
- Play Simon says.
- Play follow the leader.
- Play tug of war.
- Set up relay races.
- Jump on a trampoline.
- Jump on a pogo stick or hoppity-hop.
- Ride an exercise bike.
- Ride a sit-n-spin toy.
- Swim.
- Play sports.
- Learn karate or other martial arts.
- Learn to jump rope.
- Play hopscotch.

Chapter 3

PROMOTING FINE MOTOR SKILLS

RELATIONSHIP TO LEARNING

The development of **fine motor** skills is a critical need for young children in order to establish success and independence in their performance of common daily activities. Fine motor skills are those that require using the small muscles located in the hands, mouth, and eyes, and they develop most rapidly in early childhood. Fine motor skills are continually refined into the adult years as an individual gains repeated practice both in performing familiar daily activities, such as using a keyboard or using a knife in the kitchen, and also in learning new skills that may be required of an individual's personal situation, job requirements, or recreational interests.

When children first enter kindergarten, they are already expected to have mastered controlled use of a pencil, scissors, or crayon, and in fact they spend surprisingly large portions of their day engaged in activities that require these skills. Children who struggle with fine motor skills are at a distinct disadvantage for experiencing success in their early school years. They may be slow to complete assignments, avoid challenging work, especially those involving paper and pencil, and become easily frustrated. Teachers may consider them to be less competent learners than they really are, because they may have a hard time showing what they know using paper and pencil. Commonly, children who struggle with fine motor skills also experience a poor self-image because they are well aware that they are having difficulty performing certain activities as well as other children.

Besides the typical school-related fine motor activities, many other daily functions are also impacted by fine motor skills. Self-care independence relies on the child's ability to manipulate buttons, zippers, or snaps during dressing; to open food containers and use utensils without spilling when eating; and to learn to brush teeth and wash one's face and hands to maintain hygiene. Learning to read requires coordinated use of the small muscles surrounding the eyes in order to scan from left to right without losing one's place, to maintain visual focus on an object despite changes in head position, and to shift the eye's focus from near to far when looking from the teacher or board back to work at one's desk. Learning to speak clearly and with good coordination requires precise use of the small muscles that control the jaw, tongue, and lips. The smaller muscles involved in performing fine motor skills are often referred to as the **distal** muscles, because they are farthest away (distal) from the trunk.

HAND AND UPPER BODY STRENGTH

Developmentally, children first develop strength and control in their **proximal** muscles, which are the larger muscles located in the shoulders, trunk, and hips that underlie core strength and good posture. Strength in these muscles is necessary in order to have a stable base of support for developing refined fine motor movements. Children with low muscle tone—commonly those with autism, ADHD, or other learning differences—are especially susceptible to difficulties developing strength and stability of the proximal muscles. Surprisingly, at first glance they may appear to demonstrate good overall hand strength, as for example when asked to squeeze your finger, play tug of war, or lift a heavy tote bag using the handles. However, children with low tone and poor postural stability may be compensating for poor muscle strength in the complex muscular structures of the hand by substituting force using their shoulder and forearm muscles. They have difficulty isolating smaller hand movements from larger body movements. A close look at how they grasp and manipulate small objects reveals problems with moving small objects within the hand using only finger motion, a set of skills referred to as **in-hand manipulation**. They may commonly hold their pencil without the thumb tip touching the pencil, use scissors awkwardly, and may appear clumsy when handling small items like beads or Lego blocks. Because of this need for precision when manipulating small objects, there are more distal muscles than proximal muscles involved in fine motor control. For example, nine muscles are responsible just for controlling movements of the thumb, and six muscles (called **extraocular muscles**) control the movements of each eye.

Fine motor movements are best executed when the child has an upright posture, with feet firmly planted on the floor. The child needs sufficient strength in the shoulder and elbow to keep the arm in a stable position tucked into the side of the body, as this allows control when using the smaller muscles of the forearm and wrist. This stability is best demonstrated by the child's ability to color, cut, or manipulate small objects without a lot of observable movement in the shoulder or elbow. For best control, the wrist is held straight or in a slightly extended (tipped back) position, and with a supinated forearm (thumb facing towards ceiling and pinky finger pointed towards the table), which creates the anatomical balance necessary for opposing the thumb to the fingers with precision. With the wrist held in the proper position, the two sides of the hand are able to work cooperatively to efficiently manipulate small objects. The ring and pinky finger form the **ulnar** side of the hand, and typically curl into the palm of the hand to provide strength and stability during fine motor manipulations. The thumb and forefinger (the **radial** side of the hand) are then free to manipulate objects with control. To experience how this works, try performing a fine motor activity such as stringing small beads or putting paper clips on paper, first with poor posture and the elbow held high and the wrist bent downward (a position of poor stability), then with good posture and the elbow held in towards your side and your wrist held straight (the position of stability). You should be able to feel the difference in muscles used and ease of performance, which may help you to understand the importance of stability in developing control of motor movements.

MANUAL SPEED AND DEXTERITY

Once children develop the ability to apply a stable base of support for using their fine motor skills, they benefit from opportunities to practice and develop these skills in order to develop their **manual dexterity**, or skill and ease in using the hands. Consider what it feels like when you are learning any new skill that requires fine motor coordination, like learning to knit or to crochet. At first, you will need to consciously focus on how to perform the task, but as you practice over time, the movements become more automatic, and as a result, much faster. Children with poor motor planning ability struggle to learn how to perform movements automatically, or to apply learned skills to new situations (for example, tying bows on packages after learning how to tie their shoes), and are often slower than other children in completing fine motor activities. For this reason, many tests of fine motor skill use speed as an overall measure of fine motor skill. Most children are competitive by nature, and their natural drive to compete and win can be an effective tool for motivating them to practice fine motor skills. Children love to see if they can "beat" a parent or other child in simple activities like stringing a selected number of small beads, or flipping pennies from heads to tails. This is a great way to encourage practice of fine motor skills.

EYE-HAND COORDINATION

Eye-hand coordination refers to the use of visual and proprioceptive information to guide and direct the hands when performing fine motor activities. In order to successfully manipulate an object with the hands, the eyes must first locate the object to be manipulated, and provide basic information about its shape, size, texture, and weight in order for the person to know where to grasp the object, and with what amount of force or strength to grasp without breaking or dropping the object. This is sometimes referred to as **feedforward**, referring to the sensory information that will predict precisely what movements will lead to success in performing the desired fine motor activity. Once the hand has made contact with the object, visual feedback combined with tactile and proprioceptive feedback allows the individual to adjust their grasp or manipulation of the object in order to accomplish the intended task. Often, fine motor activities that require eye-hand coordination also require an element of **perceptual reasoning** (as, for example, when using a pencil to solve a maze or to copy pictures from a model), or timing (as when bouncing and catching a ball).

Common signs of difficulty with fine motor skills include:

- slow to achieve fine motor milestones (see Table 1.1)

- fails to demonstrate a consistent hand preference for skilled tools (pencil, scissors) before starting kindergarten

- shows limited interest in, exhibits frustration with, or avoids age-appropriate fine motor activities such as drawing, coloring, cutting

- uses unusual patterns of grasping a pencil or scissors

- drops small items frequently

- overly depends on adult assistance for common daily living activities, such as opening food containers or managing clothing fasteners

- has poor speech articulation

- seems unusually messy when eating

- drools or has difficulty chewing or swallowing without spilling food from mouth

- demonstrates poor handwriting compared to same aged peers.

FINE MOTOR ACTIVITIES

1 RAINBOW WRITING

Primary learning focus

- Eye-hand coordination, perception, auditory processing.
- Tends to be a calming and organizing activity.

Materials needed

- Writing surface, preferably large.
- Writing utensils of different colors (crayons, markers, sidewalk chalk).

Description

This is a fun activity for teaching young children to recognize differences between the various strokes used when forming letters. Draw a long line across the top and bottom of the paper (or use a chalkboard or whiteboard), to represent the lines on handwriting paper. Teach the child to make a row of strokes from left to right across the page while saying the name of the stroke (for example, "down, down, down" or "slide up, slide up, slide up"). Then trace the same strokes using a different color each time. The common strokes include: down, up, slide down (left to right diagonal), slide up (left to right diagonal), under ("U" shape), over (inverted "U" shape), and across (horizontal stroke). Larger paper and larger strokes provide more movement and sensory feedback than working in a smaller space, and may better reinforce learning. Once the child has mastered basic strokes, increase the challenge by creating multi-step patterns to follow, for example: "slide up, slide down, go across." After the child has learned the basic strokes, transfer this skill to regular, lined writing paper, and use the words to reinforce how to make the correct strokes for forming letters of the alphabet.

Variations

- For the younger child who may be confused about where to start, use colored lines or dots to provide a cue (green means "go" and red means "stop").

- Create a middle horizontal line with dots or dashes to teach the child size concepts (for example, "big down, little down").

- Perform while belly lying to increase strength and body awareness.

- Have the child close eyes or wear a blindfold while the adult holds the child's hand to draw the pattern; the child must use words to describe the strokes.

2 BEAT THE CLOCK

Primary learning focus

- Fine motor strength, dexterity, eye-hand coordination.

Materials needed

- Stopwatch or watch/clock with second hand.

- Assorted fine motor challenges that can be timed, for example:
  - Flipping ten pennies from head to tail.
  - Stringing ten beads on a shoelace.
  - Putting five paper clips on an index card.
  - Using tweezers to put ten buttons into an empty pill bottle.
  - Using a hole puncher to make ten holes in an index card.

Description

This is a very motivating way to help children to track their own progress as they develop and refine their fine motor skills. Create a "kit" of activities (aim for at least eight to ten) that are suitable for the particular challenges of the child. Then, provide directions for each activity, say "ready, set, go," and begin timing each activity. At the end, add up the total amount of time used for each activity to create the child's "score." Repeat this game periodically to see if the child can "beat" her record. Many children enjoy keeping a chart or record of their speed so that they can track their improvement over time.

Variations

- Infinite variations are possible depending on what skills are challenging for the child—try to include some skills that are very easy and fun, along with several that are more challenging.

◼ 3 SUNCATCHERS

Primary learning focus

- Fine motor strength, dexterity, eye-hand coordination.

Materials needed

- Thin cardboard (a file folder works well).
- Clear contact paper.
- Tissue paper in different colors.
- Permanent marker.
- Scissors.

Description

Help the child to decide what shape they would like for their suncatcher, such as a flower or balloon shape. Draw a 10cm to 15cm (4" to 6") shape on the cardboard, and cut it out to make a template of the shape the child has selected. Next, help the child to cut or tear tissue paper into very small pieces, just over 1cm (about ½") in size, and place these in a bowl. Cut out two squares of contact paper a little bit larger than the template. On the plastic side of one piece of contact paper, help the child to trace the shape template using a marker. Peel off the paper backing, and place the contact paper on the table, sticky side up (the shape will be visible through the clear contact paper). Instruct the child to place tissue paper pieces, one at a time, onto the sticky paper until the entire shape is filled in (it's OK if paper pieces overlap one another or go outside of the line—this actually creates a really interesting contrast when the finished suncatcher is held up to a window). When the shape is completely filled with tissue paper bits, peel off the paper backing on the other piece of contact paper, and place it sticky side down over the child's creation, making a "sandwich." The child then cuts out the shape on the marker line. When placed in a sunny window, the suncatcher will glow like a stained window.

Variations

- Holiday themes are especially suitable for this activity, like an egg for Easter, a shamrock for St Patrick's Day, or a pumpkin for Halloween. Children can often be motivated to make multiple suncatchers to make as gifts for friends or relatives, giving themselves more opportunity for practice with developing their fine motor skills.

• If desired, you can use pieces of construction paper to add details for the picture, for example facial features on a pumpkin in order to make a jack-o-lantern. These pieces should be placed on the contact paper first, before the tissue paper, so that they stand out in the finished product.

• Give directions for the child to follow a color pattern when placing tissue pieces to challenge auditory memory.

▓ 4 PAPER SNOWBALLS

Primary learning focus

• Fine motor strength, dexterity, eye-hand coordination.

Materials needed

• Old magazines or catalogues ready for recycling.

Description

The child and a partner each have one magazine to work from. Rip out a designated number of pages (maybe ten). Then, each partner must place one hand in a pocket or behind her back, and using only one hand must crunch up the paper to make a dense ball. This requires considerable motor planning, hand strength, and dexterity. When all of the balls are completed, say, "ready, set, go" and have a snowball fight (or throw balls at a designated target).

Variations

• Practice making balls with both the dominant and the non-dominant hand.

• Vary the weight and texture of the paper—for example, tissue paper may be more acceptable for the child who has weak hand strength or who dislikes the feel of sturdier paper.

• Throw balls at targets (for example, empty shoe boxes) that are placed around the room to provide practice in throwing near versus far, or aiming at targets across the midline of the body.

• Use a set of non-breakable mixing bowls, and assign different point values for each bowl, so the child can practice adding up her score.

▎ 5 WINDMAKERS (SEE APPENDIX B FOR DIRECTIONS)

Primary learning focus

- Fine motor strength, eye-hand coordination, visual attention, and tracking.

Materials needed

- Assorted, empty squeeze bottles (for example, ketchup or mustard squeeze bottles, an infant nasal aspirator, or empty nasal spray bottles).
- Permanent markers for decorating bottles (optional).
- Cotton balls, small pompoms, or small pieces of tissue paper.

Description

Clean and dry bottles well before using. Then decorate as desired, for example, making the bottle into an animal or creature, using the spout as the animal's "nose." Next, the child and a partner sit across a table from each other, and use the bottle to "blow" a lightweight ball across the table. The child must try to score a goal by blowing the ball off the table before her opponent can blow it back.

Variations

- Play this game while belly lying on the floor to build strength and body awareness in the trunk and upper body.
- Make a simple obstacle course, and provide verbal directions to get to the end point.
- Set up two goals at the far side of the table, and have the child hold two windmakers (one in each hand), to see which hand can more accurately reach the goal.
- For a tactile experience, put small pompoms or confetti on the child's arms or legs and use the windmaker to blow them away.

▎ 6 GO FISHING

Primary learning focus

- Eye-hand coordination.
- Easily adaptable to challenge gross motor or perceptual skills.

Materials needed

- Stick or dowel approximately 60cm (2 feet) long.

- String or twine approximately 60cm (2 feet) long.
- Small magnet.
- Index cards.
- Paper clips.

Description

Secure the string to one end of the stick, with the magnet attached to the other end of the string. Have the child draw fish or other simple figures on the index cards, and then attach a paper clip to each index card. The child then uses the fishing rod to pick up the index cards.

Variations

- Create cards that include concepts the child is learning, such as colors, letters of the alphabet, or sight word vocabulary.
- Have the child practice fishing while on an unstable surface, such as a sofa cushion, T-stool, or yoga ball.
- Start by holding the rod with both hands together, then try it with the dominant hand alone, then the non-dominant hand to challenge bilateral integration and motor planning skills.
- Make a smaller version of the fishing rod, substituting a paper clip hook for the magnet, and small plastic fish (cut from thin plastic or Styrofoam) with holes cut near the head. Float the fish in water and attempt to catch with the hook.

▌ 7 THE MARSHMALLOW FACTORY

Primary learning focus

- Dexterity, eye-hand coordination, perception.

Materials needed

- Mini marshmallows.
- Toothpicks.

Description

Connect marshmallows with toothpicks to create all sorts of buildings or other structures.

Variations

- Instruct the child to copy a design modeled by the adult, with the model in sight, then hidden to improve memory skills.

- Use the toothpicks to make letters of the alphabet.

◼ 8 SECRET ENVELOPES (SEE APPENDIX B FOR DIRECTIONS)

Primary learning focus

- Fine motor strength, dexterity, eye-hand coordination.

Materials needed

- Assorted envelopes (it is fine to use recycled envelopes—just use tape to close them up as needed)—see Appendix B for directions.

- Wide-lined markers or masking tape.

- Stickers, small treats, or index cards.

- Computer mousepad, washcloth, or sponge (optional).

Description

This is a great way to practice cutting for the child who is challenged by using scissors. Prepare the game by placing one sticker or small treat inside each envelope, then taping it closed. Make sure the sticker or treat is at one end of the envelope. On the other end of the envelope, draw a line (straight, waving, angled) for the child to cut open to obtain the reward.

Variations

- For the child who cuts while holding their scissors upside down, use a computer mousepad, a coaster, or a folded washcloth as a "launchpad" for resting the pinky side of the hand so the thumb remains facing the ceiling.

- Use strips of masking tape instead of a marker to increase tactile feedback during cutting.

- Instead of treats, insert exercise "messages" written on index cards inside the envelopes, for example, "hop five times."

■ 9 TAP THE BALL (SEE APPENDIX B FOR DIRECTIONS)

Primary learning focus

- Eye-hand coordination, strength, bilateral integration, motor planning, perception.

Materials needed

- Lightweight plastic ball (such as a whiffle ball) attached to a string approximately 60cm (2 feet) long.
- Rod or stick approximately 60cm (2 feet) long (empty wrapping paper tubes work well).
- Markers or different colored plastic tape.

Description

Prepare the rod by using markers or tape to create three different colored lines, one around the center of the rod, and one approximately 15cm (6") from each end of the rod. Next, suspend the ball from a tree branch or door sill so that it hangs approximately at the child's eye level. Instruct the child to hold both ends of the rod, and gently tap the ball on the middle line so that the ball does not bounce or bobble. When the child can do this well using the center line, try tapping with one of the end lines. This requires considerable attention as well as motor planning skill and bilateral integration.

Variations

- Instruct the child to tap out a pattern using the colored lines, such as red, blue, red, blue, without losing control of the ball.
- Tap out a pattern while skip counting or reciting the alphabet.

■ 10 BUBBLE BLASTER

Primary learning focus

- Fine motor strength, eye-hand coordination.

Materials needed

- Empty spray bottle with trigger handle.
- Bubbles (see Appendix B for a homemade recipe).
- Bubble wand (you can make your own with wire or a coat hanger).

Description

This is a great outdoor activity for a warm summer day! Fill the bottle with clear water, and then let the child try to pop bubbles by squeezing the trigger.

Variations

- Use shaving cream on a beach ball to make shapes or pictures, then use the spray bottle to clean off the beach ball.
- Use the spray bottle to try to propel a ping-pong ball to a target.
- Help spray plants with water.
- Add a few drops of food coloring and use the sprayer to make pictures in the snow.

▓ 11 PUTTY GAMES

Primary learning focus

- Hand strength, dexterity, tactile discrimination.
- Tends to be a calming activity.

Materials needed

- Clay, therapy putty, play-doh, etc. (see Appendix B for homemade recipes).
- Rolling pin, plastic knives, cookie cutters.
- Small objects (coins, beads, buttons, pegs).

Description

Playing games with clay or putty provides the resistance needed to develop hand strength, and also provides the tactile input that many children crave (but some dislike). Teach the child to use a rolling pin to flatten the clay, then use cookie cutters or a plastic knife to make shapes. Reshape into a ball, and hide small objects inside the clay and have the child go on a "treasure hunt" to find all the hidden bits. Roll the putty into shapes for a head and body, then add toothpicks, buttons, dry macaroni or other small objects to make an alien or animal.

Variations

- Try to find hidden bits with eyes closed.
- Roll out thin snakes to place onto pictures of shapes or letters.

- If the child strongly dislikes the feel of clay or putty, try having the child wear non-latex medical gloves at first.

12 THE TURKEY BASTER GAME

Primary learning focus

- Fine motor strength, eye-hand coordination.
- Tends to be a calming activity.

Materials needed

- Turkey baster (can substitute an infant bulb syringe).
- Bucket of water.
- Empty plastic soda bottle.

Description

This is another great outdoor activity for a warm day. Have the child dip the baster into the bucket of water to see how fast she can use the baster to fill up the soda bottle.

Variations

- Use two basters to create a relay race with a partner.
- Set up multiple soda bottles in different locations, and have the child follow verbal directions (for example, "do one squirt in the bottle next to the back door, then two squirts in the bottle under the picnic table").
- Instead of a turkey baster, use a sponge to soak up the water and then squeeze into the bottle to build even greater hand strength.

13 THE MUNCHER MAN (SEE APPENDIX B FOR DIRECTIONS)

Primary learning focus

- Hand strength, eye-hand coordination.

Materials needed

- Tennis ball.
- Sharp razor knife.
- Permanent markers.
- Small objects (beads, buttons, pompoms, plastic letters).

Description

Prepare a muncher man by slicing a 6cm to 8cm (2½" to 3") line along the rubber seam that separates the fuzzy parts of the ball. This becomes the muncher's "mouth." Use a red marker to draw lips around this cut, then adding eyes, nose, and any other desired facial details. The child holds the tennis ball in her palm with the thumb next to one side of the mouth, and the other fingers next to the other side of the mouth. By squeezing hard, the muncher's mouth will open so that the child can "feed" it small objects.

Variations

- Create relays, where the muncher "eats" something, then the child performs an exercise (for example hopping or skipping across a room to allow the muncher to "spit out" the food into a bowl (children love making gagging noises when they do this).

- Use magnetic letters or alphabet beads to have the muncher eat letters to form simple words.

- Instruct the muncher to eat a sequence of objects (for example, if using colored pompoms, "eat a red strawberry, then a blueberry, then a yellow lemon").

■ 14 GRABBER GAMES

Primary learning focus

- Fine motor strength, dexterity, eye-hand coordination.

Materials needed

- An assortment of tools requiring a pinch to pick up small objects (such as tweezers, strawberry hullers, squeeze-type hair clips, squeeze-style clothespins, or one-piece practice chopsticks).

- Small objects (such as beads, plastic bugs or spiders, small pompoms.

Description

Spread out objects on a table and have the child select a grabber. Use the grabber to pick up items and place them in a container. Combine different objects into a messy pile, and then have the child sort different objects into different containers, which can also challenge visual figure-ground perception. This can easily be made into a relay race type of challenge.

Variations

- Use alphabet cereal to identify (then eat) letters or short words.

- Use grabbers instead of fingers to move game pieces around a playing board.
- Use clothespins or hair clips to pinch onto objects around the room, then go on a treasure hunt to collect the items.
- Hang a string across a room and use clothespins to clip artwork for display.
- Use grabbers for a special snack using food cut into tiny bites.

15 AIR TRAFFIC CONTROLLER

Primary learning focus

- Fine motor strength, dexterity, eye-hand coordination.

Materials needed

- Blank computer or drawing paper.
- Crayons.
- Target (wastepaper basket, laundry basket, or large cardboard box with a hole cut in one side).

Description

Each player chooses a designated number of pieces of paper, and decorates the paper in a way that will identify who it belongs to—this might mean that one player decorates using blue and green, while another player uses red and yellow, or possibly one player draws fish and another player draws dinosaurs. Teach the child how to fold paper to make airplanes (younger children will need help with this). Then, players stand 2.5m to 3m (8 to 10 feet) away from the target and throw their airplanes, attempting to hit the target.

Variations

- Try making airplanes with smaller pieces of paper—these will take more dexterity to fold, and will also fly faster.
- Place multiple targets at different distances to require adjusting how hard or softly to throw the airplane.

16 BOTTLE BOWLING

Primary learning focus

- Fine motor strength, eye-hand coordination, motor planning.

Materials needed

- Ten empty large plastic soda bottles.
- Water or sand.
- Masking tape or sidewalk chalk.
- Medium-sized playground ball.

Description

Use small bits of masking tape or sidewalk chalk to mark out where the bowling pins will be placed, and to make a starting line about 3m (10 feet) away from the pins. Fill each bottle with an inch or so of water or sand, and replace the tops so the bottles will not leak. Then have the child stand on the line and try to roll the ball to knock down the pins.

Variations

- Fill bottles with more sand or water to require more force to knock down the pins and to make them heavier to set up (this will increase the amount of proprioceptive input involved in the game).
- Mark the bottles in some way (draw shapes or letters on each bottle, or fill with water colored with food coloring) and create a "code" for tallying points (for example, red pins get one point, green pins get two points, etc.).

■ 17 BUBBLE WRAP

Primary learning focus

- Fine motor strength, eye-hand coordination, bilateral integration.

Materials needed

- Bubble wrap.

Description

Children absolutely love to pop the bubbles in bubble wrap! Give the child small pieces of bubble wrap to pop as a warm-up before other fine motor activities, or cut out two squares of similar size, and have a race to see who can pop their bubbles first. Remember that larger bubbles are easier to feel and pop than smaller bubbles.

Variations

- Use a permanent marker to place small colored dots on the bubbles to make a shape or letter, then have the child pop only those bubbles that form the shape.

- Try to pop all of the bubbles while eyes are closed.

- Incorporate larger bubble wrap into obstacle courses so children can hear the pops as they maneuver the course.

- Use large packing bubbles to practice jumping skills—have the child stand on a bottom step or sofa cushion, then jump down to pop the bubble.

■ 18 RUBBER BAND BALL

Primary learning focus

- Fine motor strength, dexterity, motor planning, eye-hand co-ordination.

- Making the ball tends to be calming (but playing with it tends to be energizing).

Materials needed

- Page from a newspaper.

- Large number of rubber bands (elastics).

Description

Teach the child to start by crumpling the newspaper into the tightest ball possible. Then, start wrapping the rubber bands around the ball as tightly as possible, maintaining the round shape. Stop when the ball reaches about 4cm to 5cm (1½" to 2") in diameter. The child will be surprised by how high this type of ball can bounce!

Variations

- Play various throw, bounce, or catch games using the ball.

- This can make a good fidget toy, as the child can remove and replace bands while listening to a story or riding in the car.

- Place a series of tall targets, such as wastepaper baskets, at different distances from the child, and practice seeing how hard the ball needs to be bounced to reach different targets.

◼ 19 TISSUE ART

Primary learning focus

- Fine motor strength, dexterity, eye-hand coordination.

Materials needed

- Index cards with a simple outline (for example, ice cream cone, flower, dinosaur).
- Colored tissue paper cut into about 1cm (½") squares.
- Non-toxic glue.

Description

For this challenging art activity, the child must spread glue inside the outline, then take one piece of tissue paper at a time, and roll it into a tight ball using the thumb and forefinger. Use these balls to fill in the outline to make a three-dimensional art design.

Variations

- Instead of tissue paper, use small pieces of sponge or cotton swabs to dip into paint and fill in the outline.
- Use tweezers or other "grabbers" to pick up the tissue balls and place them in the outline.

◼ 20 CUTTING SANDWICHES

Primary learning focus

- Fine motor strength, dexterity, eye-hand coordination, bilateral integration.

Materials needed

- Two pieces of heavy duty cardboard cut in the same size and shape—these can be shaped like a piece of bread, or like any other shape that appeals to the child.
- Paper (computer, construction, anything you have).
- Scissors.
- Metal binder clip.

Description

Place a piece of paper between the two cardboard shapes (this is the "filling" for the sandwich), making sure that the shapes match up. Secure firmly with a binder clip. Have the child cut around the shape using scissors, cutting off any of the filling that spills out of the shape. For many children who avoid using scissors, this is a motivating activity that really draws their attention.

Variations

- Place a computer mouse mat or a folded washcloth for the hand holding the scissors to rest on—this can help keep the forearm in the correct position during cutting.

- Add extra pieces of paper (pretend they are lettuce or tomatoes)—cutting through multiple layers requires greater strength and motor planning.

- Once the child gets the hang of it, try removing the binder clip so the child has to hold the pieces together without any help.

■ 21 HAUNTED HOUSE

Primary learning focus

- Fine motor strength, dexterity, eye-hand coordination, motor planning.

Materials needed

- A large cardboard box.
- Razor cutter or razor knife.
- Markers or crayons to decorate the house.
- Paper (newspaper or magazine pages work well).
- Paper towels or tissues.
- String.

Description

First, use the knife to cut windows and doors in the haunted house. Then let the child decorate the house. Encourage creativity—and demonstrate how to make cobwebs or bats for the child to copy. Assemble materials to make "ghosts," including the newspaper, towels or tissues, and 15cm (6") lengths of string. Take the pieces of newspaper or magazine paper and crumple them into tight balls. Place each ball in the center of the towel or tissue, and teach the child how to tie a simple overhand knot tightly around the ball to make a ghost. This is a good way to introduce tying for the child who cannot yet tie shoelaces. Play games throwing the ghosts into the windows and doors of the haunted house.

Variations

- Experiment with different materials to make ghosts smaller, larger, heavier or lighter.

- Place the haunted house farther away, or up on a table, to make it harder to play.

22 PUSH-INS

Primary learning focus

- Fine motor strength, dexterity, eye-hand coordination.

Materials needed

- Assorted empty containers with plastic lids (for example, coffee cans, Pringles containers, or empty film cans).

- Razor knife.

- Assorted small objects (coins, marbles, toothpicks), choosing a different type of object for each can.

Description

Place objects in containers according to size (for example, marbles would fit well in a coffee can, coins in a small Pringles container, toothpicks in a film canister.) Use the knife to cut an opening in the lid just large enough to insert the objects (small X for the marbles, a slit for the coins, small hole(s) for the toothpicks). Empty the contents of one container into a small bowl, and instruct the child to pick up items one at a time and transfer to the palm of their hand. See how many objects the child can hold before she starts to drop the items—this takes a great deal of skill with in-hand manipulation skills. Then, let the child practice inserting the items one at a time into the container.

Variations

- Create matching containers, and try using both hands simultaneously.

- Try it with eyes closed to increase sensory feedback.

- Have the child sit on a T-stool or yoga ball, then roll marbles for the child to catch and insert into the can.

▮ 23 BUTTON SNAKE (SEE APPENDIX B FOR DIRECTIONS)

Primary learning focus

- Fine motor strength, dexterity, eye-hand coordination, motor planning, bilateral integration.

Materials needed

- 8cm (3") pieces of felt or fleece cut in rectangles or ovals (different colors).
- Scissors.
- Buttons (all the same size), needle, and thread.

Description

Sew a button on the end of each felt or fleece piece, and cut a slit (the buttonhole) at the other end. Let the child practice buttoning pieces together to make a pet snake.

Variations

- Use snaps instead of buttons.
- Sequence the size of buttons and pieces of felt or fleece from larger to smaller.
- Instruct the child to assemble the snake according to a color pattern.
- Use pieces of thin cardboard (for example, from a file folder), punch a hole in each end using a hole puncher, and assemble with copper paper fasteners (brads)—children love to color or decorate these snakes.

▮ 24 HOMEMADE RING TOSS

Primary learning focus

- Eye-hand coordination, motor planning.

Materials needed

- Lid from a large cardboard box.
- Markers or crayons for decoration.
- Empty spools of thread.
- Hot glue gun.
- Chenille pipe cleaners to form rings.

Description

Glue empty spools onto the inside of the cardboard box lid. Write numbers under each spool to indicate the point value. Decorate as desired (for example, make it a space game by drawing stars, moons, or planets around each spool). Form rings by twisting the pipe cleaners together. Start by trying to toss rings while the ring toss is placed flat on the floor. A more difficult challenge is to throw rings onto the spools while the ring toss is propped up on its side.

Variations

- Place the ring toss at one end of a balance beam or taped line, with rings placed at the other end — instruct the child to pick up one ring at a time, walk the beam, then throw at the target.

- Glue more than one empty spool on top of each other to make a longer "stick" to catch the rings.

- Practice with smaller and larger rings.

■ 25 TREAT BOXES (SEE APPENDIX B FOR DIRECTIONS)

Primary learning focus

- Fine motor strength, dexterity, motor planning, bilateral integration.

Materials needed

- An empty cardboard box, such as a shoebox.

- Two shoelaces, each colored differently (thicker laces, or textured sport laces work best).

- Small candies, stickers, or other reward.

Description

This is a great activity for motivating children to practice tying their shoes. Start by punching two holes in the bottom of the box. Next, cut the shoelaces in half and tie two halves together so that you have a lace with different colors at each end. Poke the ends of the shoelace through the holes from the inside of the box (so they project outwards through the bottom of the box). Put the lid on the box, and wrap the laces around so that you can teach the child how to tie. The two different colors make it easier to learn where each lace must go, and thicker laces are easier to control than thinner ones.

Variations

- Vary the length and texture of the laces to require more motor planning skill.

- Use several boxes of different sizes so that they can nest inside one another.

- I like to place a reward inside the smallest of a nesting set of boxes, and practice tying until all of the boxes are inside of one another. Then, I engage the child in a more challenging or non-preferred learning activity, and if she is successful, they can untie all of the boxes to get their treat.

OTHER IDEAS FOR SUPPORTING FINE MOTOR SKILLS DEVELOPMENT

- Using pop beads.
- Using pegboards.
- Playing with building or construction toys, the smaller the better.
- Using spinning tops.
- Playing with wind-up toys.
- Using finger puppets for make-believe.
- Assembling crafts.
- Playing games with small parts, like Cootie or Mr Potato Head.
- Helping in the kitchen (for example, snapping beans, husking corn).
- Using stencils for tracing.
- Having a box of old clothes and accessories for dress-up.
- Dressing up dolls or stuffed animals.
- Using craft punches to make confetti or for art projects.
- Singing songs with fingerplays.
- Learning the sign language alphabet.

Chapter 4

PROMOTING VISUAL SKILLS

RELATIONSHIP TO LEARNING

Vision is commonly thought of as our "window to the world," and is critically important in all aspects of learning. Obviously, one needs to see clearly in order to learn shapes, colors, letters and numbers; to safely negotiate one's environment; to take care of daily needs like buttoning a shirt or pouring milk into a glass without spilling; or to understand whether someone's body language and facial expression means "That's a great idea!" or "Don't bother me now!" Most of the time, significant issues with **visual acuity** (seeing things clearly whether they are near or far away) or eye muscle control are identified early in childhood and managed using medical interventions or the use of glasses. However, vision plays a much more complex and dynamic role in daily life than just being able to see clearly. Using vision effectively involves paying attention to multiple simultaneous stimuli that are constantly changing in time and space, then applying meaning to those stimuli. The eyes must have sufficient muscle control to be able to work together to move and adjust focus on stationary targets as well as those that move around so that the orientation, lighting and background are constantly changing. Problems with eye muscle control, sometimes called **visual efficiency disorders**, can be very subtle and hard to detect, and can fluctuate over time. If mild or intermittent, they may not be identified during routine eye exams, because they do not affect the child's acuity, or ability to see clearly. However, such problems can cause the child to tire easily or to feel discomfort when using his eyes, especially for close-up viewing. Young children often fail to complain about symptoms of visual efficiency disorders, which may include blurring, headaches, or double vision. This is because they may not recognize these symptoms as problematic. If their eyes have always worked in the same way, they will not even consider the possibility that other children might actually see things differently.

Once the eyes transmit images to the brain, the brain must interpret the meaning and importance of those images, a process referred to as **visual perception**, or **perceptual reasoning**. Problems with visual perception involve difficulty recognizing, remembering, and organizing the visual images transmitted by the eyes to the brain. Problems with visual efficiency and visual perception are common among children with developmental differences, including those with autism, ADHD, and specific learning disabilities. Although they can vary widely among children, certain visual difficulties are predictably more associated with certain disabilities. For example, children with autism commonly avoid eye contact with others, seek intense visual stimulation such as spinning objects while ignoring stimuli peripheral to the object they are looking at, and avoid looking at their hands when manipulating objects. Some children with ADHD are believed to have difficulty maintaining close visual focus on near objects, a problem with visual efficiency, which may be why they are so easily distracted by things they see. Children with specific learning disabilities including **dyslexia** often have poor visual memory skills, or show reversals in their reading and writing. It is important to understand that activities designed to improve visual efficiency or visual perception cannot actually change the way that the brain processes information. However, activities to improve visual efficiency can make visual learning more comfortable and automatic, and can increase a child's motivation to learn. Activities to promote visual perception skills can help children to better attend to relevant visual details, to develop coping strategies for better understanding of visual information, and to experience less frustration during learning challenges.

VISUAL ATTENTION AND TRACKING

Visual efficiency skills play an important role in how easily a person can focus on various visual targets. **Accommodation** refers to the ability of the muscles surrounding the eyes to change the shape of the lens at the front of the eye as objects move closer or farther away from the eyes. When accommodation occurs correctly, the visual image remains clear, regardless of the distance from the eyes. Accommodative disorders result in unfocused vision, and exist when accommodation is less than normal, slower than normal, or cannot be sustained for the normal length of time. Typically, most young children have better accommodation ability than many adults, since adults tend to gradually lose the muscular elasticity needed for this skill. That is why many older adults need to use glasses for reading or other close work, even when they never wore glasses as a child. Problems with accommodation can make it hard to catch or throw a ball, since the eyes need to remain focused as the ball comes closer or moves farther away. Similarly, children with accommodative disorders often have difficulty shifting their vision from the teacher or board back to their desk.

Binocular vision refers to the ability of the visual system to convert the separate images received from each eye into a single visual image for the brain to process. Children who have a different level of visual acuity in each eye may struggle with binocular vision unless they wear glasses to correct their vision. Other children have problems with alignment of the eyes, also called **strabismus**. Strabismus is a common childhood problem, and can be caused by a number of factors, including abnormal focusing ability, a weakness in the eye muscles, or a disorder of the nerves controlling eye movement or in the part of the brain that controls eye movements. Strabismus causes one eye to turn in or out or upwards and can be constant or intermittent. When the eyes are misaligned, each eye sends a different message to the brain, which the brain then processes as double vision. Because the brain has trouble interpreting this double image, one of two mechanisms may occur. Sometimes, the child may be able to exert extra muscular effort to realign the eyes, at least for some period of time, a strategy that can lead to eyestrain. Alternatively, the brain can elect to ignore one of the two images, a mechanism known as suppression. When young children suppress vision in one eye, that eye no longer receives visual stimulation, which can halt the development of that eye. This is called **amblyopia**, or lazy eye, which is a serious condition that can lead to permanent vision loss if left untreated. Significant problems with strabismus are generally identified during routine vision exams, but milder problems or those that occur intermittently may go unnoticed. Problems with eye muscle control can also affect the child's ability to rapidly scan or track visual stimuli along a horizontal plane, a skill that is extremely important during reading. Children with eye tracking difficulty frequently lose their place during reading, or use excessive head movement to follow the print. If your child has had normal vision examinations, but shows any signs of visual efficiency difficulties, you may wish to seek a second opinion from an optometrist who specializes in the vision problems associated with learning differences, called a **developmental optometrist**. Several websites are described in Appendix C to learn more about what these specialists have to offer.

VISUAL PERCEPTION

Visual perception simply means understanding what is seen, and plays a critical role in all aspects of cognition and learning. These skills are part of how the brain processes information for learning, and as such, contribute to an individual's overall intelligence. Visual perception problems may co-exist with visual efficiency problems, but also commonly occur in children with normal vision. There are many different types of visual perceptual weaknesses, and different specialists may use different terminology to describe the problems. However, certain common problems are generally well understood among professionals.

Visual attention relates to a child's alertness and readiness for learning when visuals are involved. It requires conscious effort to concentrate and persist with looking. It also requires the child to notice which visual stimuli are unimportant to the task at hand, and to make a choice as to which stimuli to focus on, and which to ignore. Children with problems affecting visual attention may fail to notice relevant details in a learning task, or alternatively, may become easily overwhelmed by visual details that are better ignored. **Visual discrimination** skills are those that allow the child to recognize the basic features of an object such as color, shape, or size through sight alone. **Visual closure** refers to the ability to recognize forms or objects that are incomplete, based on relating a visual stimulus to previously learned information. This is the skill that allows a baby to recognize his bottle, even if it is partially hidden under a blanket, or for an older child to recognize that there is a good chance that the next letter after "C" and "A" will probably be "T" when reading a story about pets. Problems with visual closure often underlie poor spelling or reading abilities. **Visual form constancy** is the skill that allows the child to understand that objects and visual stimuli do not have to look exactly alike in order to mean the same thing. It is what allows the child to recognize that a two-dimensional picture of a ball means that round thing that is so much fun to throw and catch; that a fire engine seen from far away is really larger than it seems; and that a printed letter means "A" whether it is upper case or lower case, manuscript or cursive, or presented in different fonts or forms. **Visual figure-ground discrimination** helps the child to separate foreground from background visual stimuli in order to attend to relevant details. It allows the child to focus quickly on the most relevant details of an image, while retaining an awareness of the relationships of parts to the whole image. Children with poor figure-ground skills often lose their place when doing visual activities, and may benefit from books or worksheets that have fewer images per page, or that visually highlight the most relevant aspects of the materials. **Visual memory** is the ability to recall visually presented information. There are different types of visual memory, including the ability to immediately recall something right after it was seen (also called **working memory**); long-term recall of information (such as what different punctuation marks are supposed to look like); and the ability to remember the exact order of a series of stimuli, such as a telephone number (also called *visual sequential memory*). Many children with learning disabilities have problems with visual memory, especially working memory. **Visual-spatial perception** is the ability to recognize the orientation and position of objects to other objects or to oneself. It allows the child to recognize such basic concepts as left from right, up from down, top from bottom, and to learn the vocabulary associated with these concepts. Children with problems in this area often reverse letters, numbers or words beyond the age when it is developmentally appropriate to do so (up to second grade or so). They commonly have difficulty with drawing and handwriting, or with organizational skills, and may exhibit problems with higher-level math skills.

VISUAL-MOTOR INTEGRATION

Visual-motor integration is a broad term used to describe how visual perceptual information coordinates with fine motor or gross motor skills to produce an accurate and well-executed motor response to an environmental demand. It requires the child to continually adjust his movements based upon the visual information that keeps changing as the movement is executed. Visual-motor integration skills are what allow a child to connect his foot with a moving ball during soccer, to anticipate how wide to open the mouth to accept a bite of food without spilling, or to move the hand in a precise manner in order to cut on a line or color within boundaries. Children with visual-motor

74

integration problems may appear generally clumsy, and often have trouble with many school activities requiring the manipulation of pencils, scissors or other classroom tools and materials.

Common signs of difficulty with visual efficiency or perceptual skills include:

- frequently squints, rubs eyes (especially one more than the other), or gets watery eyes unrelated to a cold or allergies

- complains of aching or burning eyes, headaches, blurred or double vision, or nausea and dizziness during or immediately after close visual activities

- dislikes or avoids activities that require close visual attention

- shows difficulty concentrating or attending to activities requiring visual attention

- shows unusual sensitivity to sunlight, glare, or fluorescent lights

- has unusual difficulty throwing at a target or bouncing and catching a ball

- demonstrates poor reading comprehension despite good vocabulary and spoken language skills

- frequently loses place during reading (skips words or whole lines)

- reverses letters, numbers, or words after first grade

- poor handwriting, especially size and spacing consistency, and use of margins

- shows difficulty with math concepts such as time, money, carrying, or use of graphs

- tilts head, or closes one eye during reading

- moves whole head to follow a line of print, instead of moving the eyes independently of the head

- persistently holds books or worksheets in an unusual position

- demonstrates excessive fatigue at the end of a typical school day.

VISUAL LEARNING ACTIVITIES

■ 1 GEL BAGS (SEE APPENDIX B FOR DIRECTIONS)

Primary learning focus

- Visual attention/tracking, visual-motor integration.
- Tends to be a calming activity.

Materials needed

- Large, freezer zip-lock bag.
- Colored hair gel.
- Duct tape.
- Small bead or button.

Description

Squirt a good amount of gel in the bag (enough to fill the bag to approximately 0.6cm (¼") thickness all around). Insert the bead or button, and carefully squeeze to remove all excess air. Close the zipper and seal with duct tape to prevent leaking. This bag can be placed on top of shapes or letters to trace, dot-to-dot pages, or mazes. The child uses his index finger to push the bead in the desired path.

Variations

- Add glitter or sequins for visual contrast.
- Chill the bag in the refrigerator to create a different tactile sensation.

■ 2 POMPOM MAGNETS

Primary learning focus

- Visual attention/tracking, eye-hand coordination, visual-motor integration, fine motor strength and dexterity.

Materials needed

- Assorted colored pompoms, one size only.
- Magnets or magnet tape.
- Hot glue gun.
- Aluminum cookie tray.

Description

Use the hot glue gun to attach magnets to the pompoms. Then, use the pompoms as an art medium to create various pictures and designs on the cookie tray.

Variations

- Practice making letters and shapes with the pompoms.

- Use pompoms to reinforce number concepts, for example "how many red pompoms did you use?" or "did you use more blue pompoms or more yellow pompoms?" or "How many pompoms do you think we will need to write your name?".

- Tape a coloring shape or maze to the cookie tray, and use pompoms to color in an area, or follow a path.

- Prop the tray so it is in a vertical plane at eye level to encourage arm strength and a good hand position for maintaining a pincer grasp, or use the pompoms on a refrigerator or metal file cabinet.

- This is a good activity to perform while sitting on a T-stool or yoga ball.

◼ 3 MARBLE ROLLER (SEE APPENDIX B FOR DIRECTIONS)

Primary learning focus

- Visual attention/tracking, visual-motor integration, motor planning, bilateral integration.

Materials needed

- Marble.

- One half of a small plastic Easter egg, or a bottle cap just large enough to fit completely over the marble. This is the "roller."

- Tray (lightweight plastic works best, but a small cookie tray or empty cardboard box top would also work well).

- Paper and markers.

Description

This activity requires using the two hands together while focusing visually on a moving target. Considerable timing and motor planning are required to control the marble. Draw simple paths or mazes on paper (or find free printables from the internet), and then place the paper on the tray. Next, place the roller over the marble and place it on the tray so it can roll around. If desired, the child can decorate the bottle cap to make it look like an alien or animal. The child must grip the sides of the tray, and try to control the marble as it moves along the path.

Variations

- Make a paper that has numbers or letters of the alphabet scattered around; the child must count, recite the alphabet, or spell simple words while rolling the marble to the correct location.

- Try this with a partner, having each partner hold one side of the tray and work together to control the marble.

- Call out verbal directions (one at a time, or a sequence of several directions) for the child to follow as quickly as possible.

- Use masking tape on a linoleum floor to mark out a basic shuffleboard course, and use the marble roller to slide to designated areas in order to earn points—this is a good way to learn how to control the force of movement, which helps to develop proprioceptive awareness.

■ 4 MY COLOR BOOK

Primary learning focus

- Perceptual, eye-hand coordination, dexterity.

Materials needed

- Construction paper in different colors.
- Stapler or other method for assembling a book.
- Old magazines or catalogues.
- Glue stick, scissors.

Description

This is a great rainy day activity! Assemble a book with different colors for each page. Allow the child to decorate a cover for their book. Then, allow the child to search through magazines to find objects of different colors, cutting and pasting them on the correct page. This is an activity that can be done in one day, or work on it a little at a time over several days.

Variations

- Create other category books, for example shapes, types of animals (pets, zoo, forest, farm), or food categories (meats, vegetables, grain, dairy, desserts). Put one example of the category at the top of each page.

▦ 5 PADDLE BALL (SEE APPENDIX B FOR DIRECTIONS)

Primary learning focus

- Visual attention/tracking, eye-hand coordination, motor planning.

Materials needed

- One or more paddles.
- Balloons, ping-pong balls.

Description

Use a paddle (such as those used for ping-pong) or make your own by bending a metal coat hanger into an oval with a handle, stretch a used leg from pantyhose over the oval, wrap the handle with foam or cloth, then cover the handle with duct tape to hold it all together. Teach the child to hold the paddle flat and to practice tapping a ball, making sure that he keeps their eyes on the ball. Start with something that moves slowly and is easy to hit (like bubbles), next try it with balloons, and finally try it with a fast-moving ping-pong ball. Children love to keep track of how many times they can hit the ball without letting it fall to the ground.

Variations

- Use paddles to hit a balloon back and forth with a partner.
- Let the child hold one paddle in each hand and tap back and forth with one hand, and then the other.
- With a partner, paddle a ball back and forth on the floor while standing, kneeling, or sitting on a T-stool or yoga ball.

▦ 6 HIDE AND SEEK FOR THE EYES

Primary learning focus

- Visual attention/tracking, figure-ground perception.

Materials needed

- A collection of small objects, for example, 10 beads, or 15 paper clips—anything you happen to have around the house.
- A paper bag or small bowl for "collecting" the items.

Description

Have the child start by counting the number of objects so he knows how many things to find for a treasure hunt. Next, teach the child that this will be a treasure hunt for the eyes alone—nothing will hide inside of or underneath anything else, and nothing will be too high for the child to reach without climbing on anything. This is also a time to teach about any areas that might be "off limits" (for example, when I play this game at school my students know that nothing will be hidden on my teacher's desk). Then, have the child cover his eyes while you hide the objects. When ready, give the child a small bag or bowl and let them find the items, giving clues as needed (such as "you are getting warmer!").

Variations

- I always hide one item on my person, which is especially useful for encouraging children with autism to make eye contact and really connect with another person.

- Have the child remain seated and find the objects with eyes only, telling you where each item is so that they have to practice using expressive vocabulary.

- Children love doing this activity on holidays, using theme-based materials, such as stickers, or small Easter eggs. At Easter time, I hide a small carrot or two and make a big fuss about the Easter bunny being nearby; at Christmas I hide one or two small pieces of doll clothing that I have made out of felt, or a scarf that I have knitted using fine wool and toothpicks (obviously misplaced by one of Santa's elves).

- Use pinch-style clothespins or hairclips clipped onto curtains or other likely places, so that children have to use their fine motor skills when searching.

- Make it an auditory perceptual game by asking "Where am I now?" as you move about the room to hide objects.

■ 7 FLASHLIGHT TAG

Primary learning focus

- Visual attention/tracking, visual-motor integration.

Materials needed

- Two narrow-beam flashlights.

Description

Sit behind the child in a darkened room, facing a blank wall. Draw lines, trails or paths for the child to follow with his flashlight, starting with slow movements in a small area, and gradually moving faster and over a wider area.

Variations

- Take turns drawing shapes or letters while the other person guesses.
- Use a laser pointer instead of a flashlight to make shapes or letters that the child must guess—the laser pointer makes a clearer image, but be very careful not to shine it near the child's eyes, as this could be harmful.

▦ 8 TOOTHPICK TUNNEL

Primary learning focus

- Visual attention/tracking, eye-hand coordination, perception.

Materials needed

- Cylinder of various sizes (toilet paper tube, empty towel roll, fat drinking straw).
- Two toothpicks.

Description

Give the child two toothpicks, one to hold in each hand. Hold the cylinder horizontally in front of the child, and see if he can insert both toothpicks simultaneously in and out of the cylinder while you move it closer or farther away. This requires a great deal of coordination and depth perception.

Variations

- Try it while sitting or standing on an unstable surface.
- Tilt the cylinder at various angles to increase the challenge and require greater depth perception.

▦ 9 PUFF BALL

Primary learning focus

- Visual attention/tracking, motor planning.
- Tends to be a calming activity.

Materials needed

- Drinking straw.
- Cotton ball, pompom, or small pieces of tissue paper.

Description

Sit across a table from the child, placing the cotton or tissue in the middle of the table. Both the adult and child use a straw to try to blow the cotton off the opponent's side of the table, scoring a point. Keeping the mouth closed around the straw and blowing with control requires a great deal of oral motor input that is calming to many children.

Variations

- Have the child get on the floor on hands and knees, and use the straw to blow a ball through a maze or an obstacle course.
- Have the child suck through the straw to pick up a small piece of tissue paper and carry it to a designated area so that he can deposit it in a bowl—this can be set up as a relay race with a partner.

■ 10 THE DETECTIVE GAME

Primary learning focus

- Visual attention/tracking, perception.

Materials needed

- Recycled magazines or catalogues.
- Pencil or marker.

Description

This activity is great for helping children to learn how to sustain visual attention and to develop the tracking skills needed for fluent reading and writing. Take a page from a magazine (number of lines and size of print depend on the child's maturity). Teach the child to track each line with the eyes and to look for specified items, and then cross off each item using the pencil or marker. For example, have the child look for all of the letter "t's" or all of the words starting with the letter "b," without skipping any lines or letters.

Variations

- If you have access to a computer and printer, you can make your own pages and customize the task to the child. For example, type out a sheet of random letters, and have the child find each letter in their name in sequence, or type out random words with a targeted spelling word inserted periodically.

- Using a computer, make random rows of commonly reversed letters or words for the child who struggles with this (for example, make random lines or "b's" and "d's," or "mom" and "wow").

- Attach the paper to a clipboard so it will not slip around, then make a small "spyglass" out of cardboard for the child to hold with the non-dominant hand, checking off items with the dominant hand (this is a very challenging bilateral integration task).

- Lay the paper on a pillow or piece of Styrofoam, and let the child poke out the targeted letter or word using a toothpick.

- Using larger print pages, tape the page to a wall and have the child stand a few feet away. Using a pointer, the adult slowly tracks the lines, and the child must call out "stop" each time the targeted letter or word occurs.

▨ 11 BASIC VISUAL MEMORY GAMES

Primary learning focus

- Visual attention, perception.

Materials needed

- Cookie pan or small tray.
- Assorted small objects.
- Something to cover the tray (empty pillowcase, or large empty box).

Description

Assemble several objects on the tray (start with four or five and gradually increase the number). Have the child study the objects for a few seconds, then cover the tray and ask how many objects the child can recall.

Variations

- Have the child study the objects on the tray, then place a cover over the tray and remove one item to see if the child can remember which item is missing.

- Have the child study the objects on the tray, then place a cover over the tray and add one item to see if the child can identify what was added.

- Have the child study the objects on the tray, then place a cover over the tray, move the objects around, then see if the child can replace objects to their original position.

- Line up the objects from left to right on a strip of masking tape, cover them and change the order, and see if the child can return objects to their original order.

■ 12 PATTERN MEMORY GAMES

Primary learning focus

- Visual attention/tracking, perception, eye-hand coordination, visual-motor integration.

Materials needed

- Assorted drawing materials (paper and pencil, crayons or markers).

- Assorted materials for three-dimensional construction (for example, building blocks or Lego bricks).

- File folder or other visual barrier.

Description

The adult and child are each provided with a set of the same materials. Sit across a table from the child and draw or build something to copy. Place the file folder so that it hides the adult's model, and see if the child is able to copy the model from memory.

Variations

To work on auditory skills, the adult can leave the barrier in place while building the model, and provide verbal clues, for example, "I'm starting with a red block, then putting a blue block on top of the red block, and a green block in front of the red block"—the child copies the model by listening to the clues.

▓ 13 SPOON RELAY

Primary learning focus

- Visual attention/tracking, perception, balance, body awareness, motor planning.
- Tends to be a calming activity.

Materials needed

- Plastic spoon.
- Cotton ball, pompom, or ping-pong ball.
- Balance beam or simple obstacle course.

Description

Ask the child to balance the ball on the spoon while holding the spoon in his mouth. Then see if the child can negotiate a balance beam or obstacle course without dropping the ball. To do this, the child must frequently shift visual focus from near point (the ball) to far point (feet) in order to balance, which requires a great deal of visual focus and coordination.

Variations

- Substitute a small edible (raisin or M&M) and allow the child to eat any that make it to the end without falling on the floor.
- Have the child follow verbal directions to get to an end point (for example, take two sideways steps, then two backwards steps).

▓ 14 THE DOT MAP

Primary learning focus

- Visual attention, spatial perception, motor planning, bilateral integration.

Materials needed

- Sidewalk chalk.
- Paper and marker.
- Clipboard with clear sheet protector and wipe-off crayon or marker.
- Red and blue ribbons (optional).

Description

Draw a grid that has 25 large dots, five across and five down (or, create larger grids for older children). This will be the map (you may wish to use a computer for this, so that the dots are evenly spaced and you can print out more than one copy). Insert the map into the sheet protector and secure with the clipboard. Using the sidewalk chalk, find a large area of asphalt or sidewalk, and create a similar grid with 25 dots. Find a landmark at one end of the grid (such as a tree or swing set) and teach the child that his feet must always be pointing towards that landmark (this will avoid spatial confusion as the child attempts to follow the map). Use the marker to draw a path on the map, and then let the child carry the map as he tries to follow the path. If needed, put a red ribbon around the child's right ankle ("r-r-red means right") and a blue ribbon around the left ankle to help the child to remember which side is which.

Variations

- Have the child hop or jump to the dots to encourage gross motor skills.

- Have the child look at the map and then try to follow the path from memory.

- Give verbal directions for the child to follow (for example, "take two steps forward, then one step backwards") and then have the child carry a blank map and try to draw lines representing the steps taken.

▌ 15 BUTTON BOX

Primary learning focus

- Visual attention/tracking, visual-motor integration, motor planning, bilateral integration.

Materials needed

- One or more empty egg cartons with the top removed.

- Markers.

- A button or other small, lightweight object.

Description

Mark each section of the egg carton with a different color or symbol (letters, numbers, shapes) leaving one section unmarked. Place the button in the unmarked section. Instruct the child to hold the egg carton with two hands and then try to flip the button to a designated location.

Variations

- Have the child try to follow a sequence, such as spelling out the letters of his name, counting to ten, or recalling a sequence of shapes or colors.

■ 16 PUZZLING

Primary learning focus

- Visual attention, perception, bilateral integration, dexterity, eye-hand coordination.

Materials needed

- Recyclable magazines with "busy" pictures.
- Ruler and marker.
- Scissors.
- Clear tape.

Description

Choose a picture for the child to study for a few moments, then turn the picture over and ask how many things they can remember. Turn back to the picture and give the child some categories of things to find, for example "blue" things, or "skinny things," or "things that are on top of something." Next, turn the picture over, and help the child to use the ruler and marker to make lines at various angles across the back of the picture. Finally, have the child cut along the lines, mix up the pieces, and tape them back together to reconfigure the picture.

Variations

- Make puzzles using artwork that has been created by the child.
- Make puzzles using mazes to see if the child can line up the paths correctly.

■ 17 WHAT'S NEXT?

Primary learning focus

- Visual attention, perception.

Materials needed

- Empty cardboard tube.

- Different colored square building blocks (or large Lego bricks).

Description
Sit facing the child, and slowly insert blocks into one side of the tube (start with only two, and build up to a longer sequence). Hold your hands over the ends of the tube, and tip it to one side, asking the child to predict the order that the blocks will come out in that side. As the child gains practice, try rotating one or more times so that they have to mentally manipulate the spatial order of items.

Variations

- Substitute toy cars, colored ping-pong balls, or other items—just make sure they are large enough that they will remain in the same order inside the tube.
- Let the child be the one to hide blocks in the tube for a good opportunity to practice bilateral motor integration.

■ 18 STRING ART

Primary learning focus

- Visual attention/tracking, perception, eye-hand coordination, visual-motor integration, dexterity.

Materials needed

- A block of wood, with small nails hammered in to make a grid (25 is a good number to start with)—or use a piece of Styrofoam with golf tees hammered in.
- Yarn, string, or ribbon of different colors.

Description
Demonstrate how to wrap the string around the nails to form different patterns. Use more than one color to make overlapping designs. Encourage the child to copy patterns you have made.

Variations

- Vary the texture of string used to increase tactile input.
- Use grids with more nails, or with nails placed closer together to increase the dexterity needed.
- Practice making letters or numbers on the grid.
- Substitute colored rubber bands (elastics) for the string or ribbon.

▉ 19 HOMEMADE LABYRINTH GAME (SEE APPENDIX B FOR DIRECTIONS)

Primary learning focus

- Visual attention/tracking, eye-hand coordination, perception, motor planning, bilateral integration.

Materials needed

- Rectangular piece of cardboard, empty cardboard box lid, or cardboard tray.
- Pre-printed large-scale maze (make your own using markers, or refer to Appendix C for ideas about where to find free printables).
- Drinking straws.
- Scissors.
- Hot glue gun or tacky glue.
- Marble.

Description

Glue the maze onto the cardboard (or draw your own). Then, use scissors to cut different lengths of straw to glue onto the sides of the paths, leaving gaps here and there to make a labyrinth. Be sure to glue straws along the edges of the cardboard as well, or place the cardboard in a tray with sides. The child holds the cardboard using two hands, and maneuvers the marble through the labyrinth.

Variations

- Use a textured surface (such as sandpaper, non-slip shelf liner, or a piece of felt) to glue the straw pieces onto—this will slow down the marble for the child who has difficulty with this activity.
- Place the labyrinth on a table or on the floor, substitute a small pompom, and have the child try to use a straw to blow the pompom through the labyrinth—this can be a very calming activity for some children.

▉ 20 HOMEMADE LACING CARDS

Primary learning focus

- Visual attention/tracking, eye-hand coordination, motor planning, dexterity, bilateral integration.
- Tends to be a calming activity.

Materials needed

- Simple shapes of familiar or favorite items (for example, fruits, dinosaurs, flowers) drawn on thin cardboard (or find printable shapes on the web and glue onto cardboard).
- Clear contact paper.
- Hole puncher.
- Long shoelace.

Description

Cover the desired shape on both sides with clear contact paper to make a sturdier lacing card. Then, use the hole puncher to make equally spaced holes around the edge of the shape (about 1cm (½") from the edge). Tie a knot at one end of the shoelace, and teach the child to "sew" around the edge using either an over-under pattern, or a whip-stitch (always going in from the top or out from the bottom of each hole).

Variations

- Many children find this a calming activity that they enjoy practicing over and over—smaller lacing cards can also make a great fidget toy!
- Punch holes in shapes made out of different textured fabrics for tactile input.
- Make lacing wheels with holes for remembering the order of the alphabet, or to use for skip counting (label or number each hole).

■ 21 MEMORY CARDS

Primary learning focus

- Visual attention, perception, dexterity.

Materials needed

- A deck of cards *or*
- Homemade memory cards (see description).

Description

This is a fresh take on the commercial memory card games that are readily available. Cards are placed face down on the table in rows, and each player turns over two cards to see if there is a match. If the cards match, that player gets to keep the cards and turn over two more, until he fails to find a match. Children love to make their own memory cards according to favorite topics or themes. I often download pictures from the web (snowflakes for winter, dinosaurs, autumn leaves) and paste them to one side of index cards to make special memory cards.

Variations

- Cut letters out of thin sandpaper and paste to index cards for a memory game; the child can trace the letters with his finger to get a tactile cue that might help to trigger the memory.

- Collect bottle caps from soda or milk bottles or water bottles, and glue tiny pictures inside the cap to make a different type of memory game requiring manipulation of small objects.

◼ 22 MAKING HIDDEN PICTURES

Primary learning focus

- Visual attention, perception, visual-motor integration, bilateral integration, motor planning.

Materials needed

- Paper and pencil.
- Colored markers or crayons.
- Simple shapes to trace around (a simple puzzle with large, non-interlocking pieces, nesting cups or mixing bowls, or even common household objects could work).

Description

Help the child to hold down an object with the non-dominant hand, then trace around that object using a pencil held in the dominant hand. Repeat with the remaining objects, making sure that the shapes overlap one another to make a confusing sort of design. Then ask the child to find and trace each shape using a different color crayon or marker, using the object as needed to check for correctness. The end product will be a colorful abstract design that most children love.

Variations

- Tracing the objects on a vertical surface increases the motor planning challenge, and is also a good way to increase shoulder and arm strength.
- Try this with smaller objects, such as different sized buttons.
- Free-draw large letters, numbers or shapes that overlap for the child to trace.

▇ 23 FINGER PALS

Primary learning focus

- Visual attention/tracking, eye-hand coordination.

Materials needed

- Two finger puppets, one for the adult and one for the child, placed on the index finger (if you don't have any finger puppets, you can draw a face on each person's index finger pad, and make a little paper hat for the finger).

Description

The adult sits facing the child, and slowly moves his puppet while the child attempts to follow, keeping approximately 15cm (6") between the puppets. Every now and then the adult says, "Give me a kiss (or hug, or high five)," signaling that the child should touch his puppet to the adult's puppet. This requires the child to rapidly shift his visual focus.

Variations

- Move the puppet in such a way as to draw a letter or shape in the air so the child has to guess what it is and copy the shape.

▇ 24 FIND-IT BAG (SEE APPENDIX B FOR DIRECTIONS)

Primary learning focus

- Visual attention, perception.
- Tends to be a calming activity.

Materials needed

- Large, sturdy plastic bag with a zipper-style closure (can substitute a clear plastic tube or empty soda bottle); if the bag has writing on it, you may be able to use lighter fluid to erase the writing.
- Two each of assorted small objects (elastic bands, beads, magnetic letters, buttons, etc.—just be sure there are no sharp points to puncture the bag)—you will need at least 25–30 sets of objects.
- Filler for hiding the small objects (for example, sand, uncooked rice, seed beads, poly beads).
- Duct tape.

Description

Fill the container or bag about half full with the filler. Then add one of each small object, reserving the matching object to keep in a separate small bag or box. Close the zipper and seal the closure with duct tape. Pull out one of the reserved objects, show it to the child, and see how quickly he can find it in the bag. This is harder than it appears, because the filler tends to cover parts of the object so that an understanding of part to whole awareness is challenged.

Variations

- To challenge auditory skills, the adult can select an object and hide it in his hand, then provide auditory clues to see if the child can find something that matches the clue. For example, the clue for a paper clip might be, "You use this to hold things together."

- Give the child a designated period of time to see how many different things he can find and write down on a piece of paper.

25 THE HOLE-IN-ONE GAME (SEE APPENDIX B FOR DIRECTIONS)

Primary learning focus

- Visual attention/tracking, eye-hand coordination, motor planning.

Materials needed

- Empty cardboard tube, such as one used for toilet tissue.
- Length of string, about 45cm (18").
- Ping-pong ball.
- Hot glue gun.

Description

Poke a tiny hole in the ping-pong ball and attach the string using the hot glue. Then, poke a small hole in one end of the cardboard tube and attach the other end of the string. The child holds the cardboard tube and tries to flip the ball up in such a way that he can catch it with the open end of the tube.

Variations

- Make two tubes, and hold one in each hand.
- Lengthen the string for increased challenge.
- Stand up three or four tubes so that they are touching, and hold them together using tape. Color the inside rim of each tube a

different color. Use only one string and ball, but have the child try to get the ball into a particular color or sequence of colors. As an added challenge, the child may need to use both hands to hold on when multiple tubes are used.

OTHER IDEAS FOR SUPPORTING VISUAL SKILLS DEVELOPMENT

- Color or paint by number.
- Where's Waldo or other hidden picture games.
- Mazes or dot-to-dot games (see Appendix C to find websites that offer free printables).
- Parquetry or pattern blocks.
- Lite-Brite.
- Etch-a-sketch.
- Puzzles.
- Perfection game.
- Construction toys, or building toy models.
- Video games that require fast action to a visual stimulus.
- Dartboards or other target games.
- Bowling.
- Miniature golf.
- Lining up dominos and then watching them fall down in a row.
- Nesting cups or dolls.
- Bingo or lotto games.
- Lite Brite toy.

Chapter 5

PROMOTING SENSORY SKILLS

RELATIONSHIP TO LEARNING

Humans are endowed with multiple sensory systems that serve to process information from the body and from the external environment in order to influence our physical activity, learning style, and emotional regulation. When most people think of the senses, they think of sight, sound, touch, taste, and smell, and have at least a general appreciation of how these sensory systems support learning. Earlier sections of this book have introduced other less well-understood sensory systems including the proprioceptive system (sensory information derived from joints and muscles that contribute to body awareness and an unconscious sense of body movement) and the vestibular system (information derived from the inner ear that contributes to balance and a sense of head position in relation to the environment or the body).

Each of the sensory systems relies on one or more organs that function as receptors for that sense. For example, the eyes are the receptor organs for sight, ears are the receptor organ for sound, and skin is the receptor organ for touch. Each of the sensory receptors are the organs responsible for transmitting sensory information to the brain, where it will be interpreted, a process known as **sensory perception**. Someone who has a disorder in one of the receptor organs, as in the case with a child who is blind or hard-of-hearing, will obviously have a difference in the way that she learns based on the disability. However, even among people who have normal **sensory reception**, there is wide variability in how an individual responds to that sensation. For example, people with well-developed sound perception might find it easier to appreciate music or to learn to recognize birdsongs than those with less developed sound perception. People with strong perceptual skills relating to vestibular and proprioceptive information might gravitate towards sports or other activities requiring balance and coordination, while those with less well-developed skills may prefer more sedentary activities.

It is rare that we need to use any one sensory system by itself. Instead, each of the sensory systems work in concert with each other to provide us with a very complex and comprehensive picture of the environment in a process called **sensory integration**. Consider this example of sensory integration at work. You are walking to a coffee shop talking to a friend, when you come to a street you need to cross. You use vision and sound to determine whether the traffic light permits crossing, and whether the traffic conditions look and sound safe. Once you determine it is safe to cross, you step off the curb leading with your right foot. Your vision and proprioception senses tell you whether your foot is aimed in the right direction so that it will land safely in the street. To maintain balance, your body will shift weight to your left leg and tilt your trunk slightly to the left to help you to maintain an upright posture. Without any conscious effort on your part, proprioceptive input from your leg and trunk inform the brain how much adjustment is not too much or too little, but just right. At the same time, you are able to remain alert to the potential dangers in the street. The sudden sound of a siren alerts you to stop walking until you determine whether you are in danger from a fire engine moving in your direction. During the whole time, you have been able to continue your conversation with your friend without distraction, maintaining eye contact while she speaks, yet scanning the environment with your eyes to make sure it is still safe to cross. You have also noticed that clouds are gathering and it looks like it might rain, and you try to recall whether you remembered to put an umbrella in your bag. For most people, those with good sensory integration skills, this process occurs naturally and without conscious thought. For others, the process works less well. Sensory messages sent to the brain are misinterpreted, and the individual finds that they must concentrate more closely on each discrete aspect of the situation, which can be very overwhelming. Problems in this area are referred to as **sensory processing disorder** or **sensory integration disorder**. Fortunately, we know that sensory integration tends to improve as a child matures, and that there are many strategies that can help a child to integrate sensory information more efficiently.

SENSORY MODULATION

Sensory experiences play an important role in shaping an individual's behavior and emotional tone. As we are continually bombarded with sensory information from our bodies and from our environment, we need to be able to attend to those sensations that are relevant to guiding our response to a situation, and tune out or ignore those that are not. This process of selectively attending to sensory experiences is referred to as **sensory modulation**. Everyone's ability to modulate sensory information varies according to different situations. For example, when you first awake in the morning, or are feeling tired or sick, you may seem lethargic and be less alert to sensory experiences. Alternatively, when you are highly excited or stressed, you may be startled or overreact to simple sensory inputs, such as someone loudly calling your name from behind your back. Consider this example. You are invited to a neighborhood party and arrive with your spouse. It is a very busy party, with loud music, children chasing each other, and neighbors calling out greetings to one other. When you first arrive, you may feel a little overwhelmed by the noise level, but after a while, your nervous system adjusts so that you can tune out some of the noise, allowing you to focus more on the congeniality of food and friendship. If you are new to the neighborhood and don't know very many people, and you arrived at the party a little late, after a very stressful day at work, and you are worried because you left your children with a new babysitter, your nervous system may take longer to adjust. If you feel more relaxed because the party is on a vacation day, and you have a close and friendly relationship with many of the neighbors, and you brought a favorite dish that you know will draw compliments, your nervous system is likely to adjust much more rapidly.

Many children with sensory integration dysfunction have problems with sensory modulation that can affect their overall arousal level and alertness to various sensations. Some children are **hyporesponsive** and need higher levels of sensory input to take notice, some children are **hyperresponsive** and over attend or become overwhelmed by normal levels of sensory input, and others show arousal levels that fluctuate from low to high. Children also show different behavioral reactions to sensory modulation difficulties. Some hyporesponsive children may appear overly passive, tired, or lethargic because they are not noticing sensory inputs that might trigger a drive to act on an environmental demand. Others may appear overly active, because they choose to seek out the sensory experiences their nervous system craves. Similarly, some hyperresponsive children appear passive because they have taught themselves to avoid situations that might expose them to potentially overwhelming sensory input. Others with hyperresponsivity are very active and lack impulse control. Their nervous system has trouble filtering sensory input, and they may incorrectly perceive some sensory experiences as threatening. To complicate things, a child may be hyperresponsive to certain sensory experiences (for example sound) but hyporesponsive to others (for example pain or temperature).

As adults, most of us have developed a number of strategies for maintaining an optimal level of sensory arousal. For example, when you find yourself falling asleep during a long car drive, you may choose to chew gum, turn on some loud music with a strong rhythm, and open the window to allow cool air to help wake you up. Alternatively, if you just finished a heated argument with your teenaged son, you may retreat to a quiet room with a warm cup of tea, and read a book while sitting in a rocker to calm your nerves. Children with sensory modulation difficulties can be taught to recognize how their body reacts to different sensory experiences, and to apply similar strategies to get their body to a calm, comfortable, and alert state. It's important to understand that everyone responds differently to a sensory experience. For example, some people are energized by loud music while others find it calming. However, we can generally predict that certain types of sensory inputs are likely to be either energizing or calming to most individuals. Table 5.1 presents examples of these. By experimenting with different sensory modifications to activities, you should be able to identify the particular sensory style of each child.

Table 5.1 Typical sensory responses

Sensory input	Energizing input	Calming input
Touch	Gentle, light touch Tickling Soft textures Unexpected touch	Firm touch or holding Hugging Firm strokes in direction of hair growth
Movement	Fast movement Bouncing, jumping Spinning or rolling	Slow movement Rocking or swaying Moving against resistance (push, pull, carry heavy objects)
Gravity	Head upright without support	Head supported by headrest, hands
Sound	Loud or exciting music Loud or sudden noise Unexpected changes in pitch or tone	Soft or gentle music Quiet, rhythmic sounds "White" noise
Vision	Bright lights or colors Objects in motion Complicated design	Indirect, low-intensity light Reduced visual distractions
Taste	Crunchy textures Salty, spicy, or sour foods	Sweet or bland foods Chewy textures Sucking through a straw
Temperature	Very hot or very cold	Warm, moderate temperature
Smell	Strong or unfamiliar odors Peppermint, cinnamon	Familiar odors Lavender, vanilla

TACTILE DISCRIMINATION AND AWARENESS

The tactile system is very large, including not only sensory receptors located in the skin, but in others throughout the body tissues located inside the body such as the lungs and digestive system. Combined with visual input, this system transmits information to the brain about size, shape, and texture. It also transmits such sensations as pain, temperature, pressure, and vibration; a feeling of emptiness meaning hunger; or a feeling of fullness indicating the need to use the bathroom. There are two different types of tactile sensations, and each type travels along a different nerve pathway to the brain. **Discriminative tactile sensations** allow an individual to precisely locate where a tactile sensation occurs. They also inform whether something feels textured like a peach or smooth like an apple, cool like a metal writing pen or neutral like a pencil, or shaped like a sphere or a cube. **Protective tactile sensations** are those that alert an individual to potential danger, as when touching something unexpectedly hot or sharp. When the brain receives this type of information, it causes the individual to rapidly move away from the potentially dangerous object.

Children who have poor tactile discrimination skills often have coordination difficulties because they are not getting enough information from the objects they touch. Getting shoes on the correct foot may be hard if they cannot feel where the arch is supposed to be, and learning to do buttons may be hard if they cannot feel the button slipping through the hole. Children with sensory modulation differences often show problems with the way that they modulate tactile information. A child who is hyporesponsive to tactile input may seem to tolerate pain or dramatic changes in temperature better than other children. She may not notice that her hands are sticky with jelly, or that her shirt is on backwards with the tag in front. Children who are hyperresponsive to tactile (often referred to as **tactile defensiveness**) overreact to typical sensory experiences. Their brain interprets common tactile experiences as very unpleasant or dangerous, even when they are not. They typically avoid situations involving tactile input, such as messy play or playing in the sand, and can become behaviorally explosive if exposed to offending inputs. To some extent, this can happen to all of us once in a while. Imagine that you are lounging at the beach, engrossed in a good novel. You feel something very light move quickly across your bare foot, and immediately jump up, thinking it is a bug or a crab, only to find that it was only a dead leaf blowing in the wind. That unexpected touch sensation had the power to trigger a strong, if brief, emotional response. Imagine the stress and discomfort when children with tactile defensiveness experience that kind of emotional reaction all day long.

AUDITORY DISCRIMINATION AND AWARENESS

Hearing is another sensory system that plays an important role in a child's learning style as well as her ability to self-regulate behavior. Many children with learning differences including autism, ADHD, or learning disabilities have **auditory processing disorders**, even though their actual hearing acuity is normal. Auditory processing disorders occur when the sounds transmitted to the brain are heard, but misinterpreted. The brain may misunderstand the specific attributes of the sound, such as the loudness of the sound, the pitch, the duration of the sensation, or the location of the sound. Many children with sensory integration dysfunction have trouble integrating all of the qualities of sounds to adequately understand what they are hearing. This can contribute to delays in learning language, and to understanding the sounds involved in forming words used in reading and writing. Children with sensory modulation difficulties may also over-or-under respond to sounds within their environment. Hyperresponsive children may appear to be easily distracted, or excessively fearful of unexpected noises. Hyporesponsive children may appear to daydream or to ignore directions offered by parents or teachers.

Common signs of difficulty with sensory processing skills include the following:

Hyporesponsivity to sensory input

- shows decreased reactions to pain or extreme temperatures

- messy during eating, unaware of spills or food on face

- shows a constant need to touch other people or objects

- fails to react when name is called

- enjoys chewing on non-edible objects, like shirt or pencil

- constantly picks or scratches at skin

- craves intense physical activity, like running, jumping, crashing—often with disregard for safety considerations

- demonstrates poor balance or body awareness

- tends to overstuff mouth, may gag or choke easily

- seems unaware of need to evacuate bowel or bladder, or fails to notice toileting accidents

- smells everything before eating or manipulating.

Hyperresponsivity to sensory input

- avoids or dislikes being hugged or kissed by familiar adults

- dislikes having face or hair washed
- seems unusually sensitive to clothing seams or tags
- avoids messy play, like glue or fingerpaints
- seems unusually picky about food odors, tastes, or textures
- over reacts to unexpected noises, like lawn mowers or fire alarms
- is intolerant of movement, dislikes being upside down, may experience motion sickness
- hesitates to take risks during play, prefers sedentary activities.

Poor tactile discrimination

- uses an unusual way of grasping pencil, scissors, fork, or other tools
- appears clumsy when manipulating small objects
- looks away from hands when engaged in skilled fine motor activities
- drops small items easily
- unable to identify the location of a gentle touch when eyes are closed
- unable to guess basic shape or texture with eyes closed.

Poor auditory discrimination

- demonstrates unclear speech, with poor articulation of sounds
- has difficulty learning to rhyme
- has difficulty hearing differences between similar-sounding words, like "duck" and "dock"
- frequently says "what" or asks for repetition when spoken to
- is easily distracted by common background noises, like a fan or water faucet
- shows delays in learning to read and write.

SENSORY ACTIVITIES

■ 1 SENSORY SEARCH

Primary learning focus

- Tactile awareness and perception, dexterity.
- Tends to be a calming activity.

Materials needed

- Deep, plastic storage container with lid.
- Sheet or cloth to place under container.
- Dry beans or uncooked rice.
- Small toys or other objects to bury in rice or beans.

Description

Many children love the sensation of placing their hands in rice or beans, and find this to be a very calming type of sensory input. Hide the toys in the container and let the child dig, explore, and play at will (placing a sheet underneath will greatly help clean-up!).

Variations

- Use kitchen tools like measuring cups, funnels, and spoons to play with—this requires that the child uses the two hands together, and can also make pleasing sounds as the rice or beans are poured from container to container.
- Hide magnetic letters of the alphabet to find which spell out the child's name or simple words.
- Try digging in the container with eyes closed and guessing what is found by feeling it.
- Play at a table while sitting on a T-stool or yoga ball.

■ 2 GOOP ON A TRAY

Primary learning focus

- Tactile awareness, visual-motor integration.
- Tends to be an energizing activity.

Materials needed

- Plastic or metal tray (cookie sheet with sides works well).

- Unscented shaving cream, hand lotion, pudding (or see Appendix B for recipes for other types of goop).

Description

This is a messy activity best done outdoors, or place a sheet or tablecloth under the tray to contain the mess. Put some goop on the tray, and let the child use it for finger-painting, or for practice in drawing shapes or letters.

Variations

- This activity offers a good opportunity for teaching the child how to isolate their index finger while curling the other fingers into the palm. If the child has difficulty doing this, try placing a pompom or small eraser in the pinky side of their palm and see if they can keep it there while they draw with their index finger.
- Add a small amount of sand or glitter to add texture.
- Sit at a table using a T-stool or yoga ball.
- Use a blender or food processor to whip up a small amount of dishwashing detergent to make "snow," then put the snow on a tray and use toy cars or plastic figures to play in the snow.

■ 3 SPAGHETTI SHAPES

Primary learning focus

- Tactile awareness, dexterity, visual-motor integration.

Materials needed

- Cold, cooked spaghetti (thicker noodles work better).
- Tray or plastic placemat.

Description

Cold spaghetti noodles make a wonderful tactile medium for making shapes, letters, or designs. Allow the child to experiment on her own, or make a model for the child to copy.

Variations

- Do this while belly lying on the floor to build upper body strength and body awareness.
- Shapes can be allowed to dry, then paint and glue to make collages or secret messages.

■ 4 RECIPE FOR A SQUEEZE

Primary learning focus

- Tactile and proprioceptive processing, body awareness.
- Tends to be a calming activity.

Materials needed

- Assorted pillows, beanbag chairs, air mattresses, yoga ball—be creative!

Description

Choose a food that the child enjoys eating, for example pizza, a sandwich, or burrito. Tell the child that you have a recipe for making that food item. Have the child lie on something soft (thick rug, mat, sleeping bag, folded blanket, or comforter) while you construct the food item by layering different ingredients on top of the child. With each ingredient, give the child a few squeezes, focusing especially on the weight bearing joints (shoulders and hips)—this provides lots of proprioceptive (deep pressure) input that many children crave and find to be calming. You may want to add condiments like ketchup or mayonnaise by massaging these on the child's arms, legs, or back, but always stroke in the direction of hair growth (stroking against the direction of hair growth can be very disregulating).

Variations

- Challenge auditory memory and sequencing by providing a verbal sequence of ingredients to layer, and then see if the child can remember the "recipe" by repeating the sequence in the correct order.

■ 5 EDIBLE CHEW NECKLACE

Primary learning focus

- Eye-hand coordination, dexterity.
- Tends to be a calming activity.

Materials needed

- Licorice laces.
- Cheerios or other loop-type cereal pieces.

Description

Allow the child to string cereal pieces onto the licorice lace to make a necklace. Assist the child in tying a knot so the necklace can be worn. Putting something in their mouth calms many children, and chewy or crunchy textures seem to be especially calming. The child can wear the necklace when working on an activity that requires concentration, and periodically bite off one or more cereal pieces to help with focus, eating the licorice after all of the cereal has been chewed off.

Variations

- Teach the child to put cereal pieces on according to a color pattern.
- Teach the child to tie a simple half-knot on the licorice lace, and alternate knots with cereal pieces.

■ 6 DEEP-SEA DIVING FOR TREASURE

Primary learning focus

- Tactile, perceptual.

Materials needed

- Deep washbasin or other container to hold water.
- Quarters, nickels, dimes, pennies (five of each).
- Non-latex medical gloves or rubber dishwashing gloves.
- Blindfold.

Description

This is another messy activity, so play it outdoors, in the tub, or with something underneath the container to soak up the mess. Place the coins in the bottom of the container, blindfold the child, and see if she can find all five of a specified coin while wearing the gloves.

Variations

- Place both hands in the water to compare sizes of different coins and to encourage bilateral integration.
- Play with a partner—each partner gets to pull out five coins, then adds up the points to see who got the most money.
- Challenge the older child to collect coins totaling a specified monetary amount, for example $.36.
- Substitute other small objects, such as magnetic letters of the alphabet to find.

■ 7 FIND THAT FINGER

Primary learning focus

- Tactile, body awareness.

Materials needed

- Paper and markers.
- Blank file folder.
- Feather, cotton swab, or pencil with eraser (optional).
- Tape.

Description

Tape the paper to the table. Next, have the child place her hands on the paper with fingers spread wide, and trace around the fingers to make a picture of the child's hands. Practice counting the number of fingers, and talk about which hand is right versus left. Next, ask the child to place hands on top of the picture while you hold the file folder under her face to block vision. Use your finger (or a feather, cotton swab, or pencil eraser) to provide a quick, light touch to one of the child's fingers. Remove the file folder, and see if the child can identify where she was touched. If correct, draw a star on the picture of that finger. See how many stars the child can collect on each finger.

Variations

- Try using two simultaneous touches, either to the same finger, or to two different fingers.
- Wearing shorts and a short sleeve shirt, blindfold the child and place a mini-sticker on different body parts, and then see if the child can feel where you placed the sticker and peel it off without looking. This is a great way to help children to stretch and reach different areas of their bodies—something very important for developing the coordination and body awareness needed to learn to dress oneself!

■ 8 DON'T SHAKE THE TABLE GAMES

Primary learning focus

- Body awareness, dexterity, eye-hand coordination, motor planning.
- Tends to be a calming activity.

Materials needed

- Extremely variable—any game or toy that requires a high level of fine motor skill.

Description

This is one of my favorite methods for teaching wiggly children to become more aware of their bodies and to learn the importance of knowing how to sit still. There are many, many commercial games that challenge fine motor skills, such as pick-up sticks, blockhead, or Jenga. These can be purchased at minimal cost, or in many cases, you can make your own (for example, use short wooden skewers to replace pick-up sticks, or pieces of Lego or any other construction toy to use as blockhead blocks). Teach the child that this is a "don't shake the table" game, and demonstrate what might happen if the table shakes (the pick-up sticks might roll, the blocks might fall). Talk about ways to avoid shaking the table (keep feet flat on the floor and hands and body away from the table unless it's your turn). Then, take turns playing the game, periodically making a mistake that shakes the table causing you to lose your turn. Teach the child that any body movement that causes the table to shake, including things like sneezes, could cause a mistake.

Variations

- Play the game while seated or standing on an unstable surface to increase the challenge.

- Play the game using the non-dominant hand, with the dominant hand held behind the back or in a pocket.

- Substitute tweezers for manipulating the game pieces.

- Use the same language for teaching body awareness and self-control during daily living activities, for example during dinner one might caution, "Be careful not to shake the table or you might spill your milk."

▪ 9 POP GOES THE FEELING

Primary learning focus

- Calming, strength, body awareness.

Materials needed

- Small paper bags, such as lunch bags.

- Stapler or tape to seal the bags.

- Paper and crayons or markers (optional).

Description

This is a good activity for helping a child to take responsibility for calming down when she is feeling angry or frustrated. When something happens to cause emotions to escalate, talk to the child about what is bothering her, then teach the child to blow that feeling into the bag and seal it up. The child can then jump on the bag to "pop" the feeling and make it go away.

Variations

- Older children can draw a picture depicting the situation that upset them and place the picture in the bag before popping it— or crush the picture into a ball and throw it into the trash can.

- Use large plastic packing bubbles instead of paper bags. Use a permanent marker to draw a face depicting the mood, then jump on the bubble to make it pop.

- For older children, substitute balloons—have the child blow up the balloon (this takes a lot of energy, and helps to calm), then let go of the balloon and watch those feelings go flying around the room as the air is released.

10 FEEL-IT BAG

Primary learning focus

- Tactile, dexterity, perception.

Materials needed

- Cloth bag or pillowcase.

- Objects to sort by touch (for example, magnetic alphabet letters, pieces from non-interlocking puzzles or shape sorters, scraps of different textured materials, common household objects such as a paperclip, spool of thread, or button).

- Bowl, tray, or empty box top.

Description

Spread the objects on a tray or other container so the child can look at what she must find. Allow the child to manipulate the various objects to get an idea of how they feel. Then, without the child looking, select one of the objects to hide in the bag. The child reaches inside the bag (no peeking — you might have to hold the opening of the bag around the child's wrist) so that she can feel it and identify what it is. This requires not only tactile perception, but also good in-hand manipulation skills to feel all surfaces of the object and move it within the hand. The ability to identify shapes by feel is closely linked to visual perception skills.

Variations

- Gradually increase the number of items in the bag, and instruct the child which one she must find—the added tactile input from multiple objects makes it more confusing to identify the specific features of an item.

- With multiple objects in the bag, see if the child can find one object and squirrel it into the palm of their hand, then find a second object without dropping the first object.

- Try finding objects with the non-dominant hand.

11 EGG TIMER ERRANDS

Primary learning focus

- Auditory, strength, motor planning, balance.

- Tends to be an energizing activity, but may calm some children who have the need to burn off energy.

Materials needed

- Egg timer.
- Stickers.

Description

This is a great way to "wake up" a child who has low energy or arousal levels. Create several fast-paced gross motor "errands" for the child to perform (for example, "Run upstairs and bring me your teddy bear," or "Here are five pieces of trash—pick up one at a time, hop to the trashcan and then throw it away"). Set the timer for an appropriate amount of time to complete the task. If the child beats the timer, she earns a high-five or a sticker.

Variations

- For the child who is slow to complete daily routines such as getting dressed in the morning, create a chart for each morning task the child must complete (for example, brush teeth, comb hair, get dressed), and let the child earn stickers or tokens to be traded for a reward when she has earned an agreed-upon number of tokens.

- Use illogical directions to encourage good listening skills, for example, "Go to Daddy's bureau, find a clean white sock, turn it inside out and put it in the freezer."

▓ 12 DIZZY DISCS

Primary learning focus

- Energizing, motor planning, balance, eye-hand coordination.

Materials needed

- Plastic lids (for example, from coffee cans or Pringles containers) to use as makeshift frisbees.
- Empty box or basket to use as a target.
- A method for spinning (sit-and-spin, swing, or swivel chair).

Description

Rotary movement (spinning) is energizing to most children, but must be used with great caution. Children who crave spinning and never seem to get dizzy can suddenly become over-stimulated, so it is very important to monitor their reactions. Never allow prolonged, unsupervised spinning, and stop immediately if the child reacts by becoming nauseated, disregulated, or sleepy. Have the child sit on the spinner, and spin moderately fast about ten times in one direction. Stop the spin, and have the child throw several discs towards a target. Then spin in the opposite direction, stop and throw. Do not prolong this game for more than five minutes or so.

Variations

- Substitute other actions for the disc throwing, for example a fine motor activity (like assembling five pop beads) or a motor sequence (clap five times, then skip to the door).

▓ 13 MY BOUNCING BALL

Primary learning focus

- Energizing, balance, strength, auditory perception.
- Can be calming for some children who need to burn off energy.

Materials needed

- Yoga ball.

- Music with a fast, well-defined beat or rhythm.
- Musical instruments (purchased or homemade).

Description

Both bouncing on a ball and listening to fast music with a beat tend to be very energizing for most children. Play music while the child sits on the ball and bounces to the rhythm (if you don't have a ball, you can substitute marching or jumping on an unstable surface). Allow the child to make movements in time to the music, or to play various musical instruments in time with the beat. Many instruments can be easily homemade. For example, fill cardboard tubes with uncooked rice or beads and seal to make shakers; use an empty oatmeal container for a homemade bongo drum; or glue two paper plates together with a few jingle bells inside to make a tambourine.

Variations

- Sing familiar songs, and experiment with speeding up or slowing down the song to see if the child can adjust her rhythm.
- Periodically stop the music unexpectedly and see how quickly the child can "freeze" her motion.

■ 14 WALL PUSH-UPS

Primary learning focus

- Strength, body awareness.
- Tends to be a calming activity.

Materials needed

- A wall (if desired, cut out a pair of handprints using contact paper and stick to the wall).

Description

Heavy work activities that provide proprioceptive input are very calming for most children. Sometimes, children just need a quick little boost to help them get ready to work on a non-preferred activity, or to get ready for a transition. This activity can be done virtually anywhere, and is a favorite of many children. If you want, place contact paper handprints on a wall or other location suitable for performing the activity (in schools, we often place a set of handprints outside of each classroom). Teach the child to stand away from the wall and place her palms against the wall (or on the handprints) with elbows extended so that the arms are straight. One foot should be slightly in front of the other, with the knee slightly bent. Keeping feet flat on the floor, slowly push in towards the wall until the nose touches the wall, then push out again and repeat ten times. Switch foot position, and repeat ten more times.

Variations

- Instead of calling them push-ups, make a game out of pretending that a wall is falling down, and the child must push against the wall to keep it from falling.

- Chair push-ups can be performed by sitting in a chair, placing palms on the chair seat under the buttocks and pushing with the arms until the buttocks slightly rise from the seat.

- Wall sit-ups can be performed by standing with the back flat against the wall, bending the knees until both hips and knees are at a 90 degree angle (with the back still against the wall), then pushing with the legs until back in a standing position.

15 DRESSING IN THE DARK

Primary learning focus

- Tactile, body awareness, motor planning, dexterity, strength.

Materials needed

- Assorted clothes (clothes that are a little too large are easier).
- Paper bags or cardboard boxes.
- Blindfold (optional).

Description

Hide a different piece of clothing in each bag or box. Line up the bags or boxes so that they are easy for the child to find. Turn out the lights, pull down the shades, and see how quickly the child can put on each piece of clothing. Turn on the lights and let the child peek in a mirror to see how well she did.

Variations

- Vary the level of demand according to the child's maturity. For example, do not expect younger children to be able to manage fasteners as easily as older children.

- Have the child try it while wearing a mitten or non-latex medical glove on one or both hands, or while wearing a blindfold.

- Make it silly—instruct the child to put clothes on backwards or inside out.

16 NAME THAT LETTER

Primary learning focus

- Tactile, perception.
- Tends to be a calming activity.

Materials needed

- Printed alphabet, or shapes drawn on paper.

Description

Sit behind the child, who is facing the alphabet or shapes. Tell the child that your finger is a "magic pencil" for drawing letters or shapes on the child's back, which the child must then guess. Pull down the child's shirt so there are no wrinkles, and use your finger to slowly draw the shape. If the child has difficulty guessing, use verbal cues to describe the letter strokes (for example, to make a letter "T" you would say "start at the top, go down, jump up, and go across"). Use the palm of your hand to erase each letter before drawing the next one (always erase by rubbing firmly downwards in the direction of hair growth, as this tends to have a calming and organizing effect).

Variations

- Let the child use chalk to draw the letter on a carpet sample instead of guessing out loud—she must then erase the letter using a different body part.
- Have the child lie down on the floor and use her body to make the letter for another person to guess.
- Have one or more partners work together to make a letter or short word for someone to guess—a great teamwork activity!

17 IF I HAD A HAMMER

Primary learning focus

- Strength, eye-hand coordination, visual attention, bilateral integration.
- Tends to be a calming activity.

Materials needed

- Age-appropriate materials for hammering (toy hammer and pegboard for toddler, golf tees and Styrofoam for older children, wooden board or tree stump and real nails for the child who can safely do this under supervision).

Description

Children (especially boys) love to use a hammer, and can amuse themselves for a long time given the opportunity! Hammering provides an excellent opportunity to practice eye-hand coordination, and provides a lot of strong proprioceptive input as well, which can be calming for some children. This is, of course, an activity that needs close supervision according to the maturity of the child.

Variations

- Use a marker to draw a picture or shape on the wood or Styrofoam, and tap in nails or golf tees staying on the line.
- Hammer according to the rhythm of a song.
- Use different colored golf tees to create a sequenced pattern.
- Hammer ice in a zipper type bag, then use the ice chips to cool down a drink.

▨ 18 BLOWING IN THE WIND

Primary learning focus

- Strength, visual attention/tracking.
- Tends to be a calming activity.

Materials needed

- Small empty milk or cream containers (clean and cut off about 4cm (1 ½") from the bottom, creating an open box).
- Craft sticks.
- Paper cut to approximately 8cm (3") square.
- Scissors.
- Tape.
- Bathtub, wading pool, or other large container of water.

Description

Tape the paper to one end of the craft stick, and tape the other end of the craft stick inside of the milk carton bottom. This creates a small sailboat that can float in water without sinking because of the waxy covering on the milk carton. Use these boats to have races, propelling the boats by blowing into the sails. Sustained blowing takes a great deal of effort, and provides calming proprioceptive input to the mouth and lungs. Experiment with how the boat moves differently if you blow soft or hard, or if you place small objects inside the boat.

Variations

- Partners can make secret messages to blow back and forth to each other, with instructions to perform a specified activity, such as acting out something, or performing an exercise.

- Experiment with other games that require sustained blowing, like bubble pipes, making and blowing into pinwheels, or using blower party favors to push a ping-pong ball around a path.

■ 19 NAME THAT TUNE

Primary learning focus

- Auditory perception.

Materials needed

- None.

Description

This is a quick and easy auditory perception game that can be done anywhere with virtually no equipment. Using your hands on your lap, tap out the rhythm of a common song, such as "Happy Birthday." You could also clap out the rhythm, or use a pencil against a hard surface. See if the child can recognize the tune.

Variations

- After the child guesses the tune, sing it together and act out the rhythm by marching, clapping hands, or snapping fingers.

- Take turns being the tapper and the listener.

■ 20 MIRROR DRAWING

Primary learning focus

- Auditory perception, visual-motor integration.

Materials needed

- Paper and markers or crayons.
- File folder or other object to use as a visual barrier.

Description

In this game, the child attempts to draw a picture that looks the same as the adult's picture, given only auditory clues. The adult and child each have paper and drawing materials. Place the file folder or other barrier in between the child and the adult, so that they cannot see each other's paper. The adult then draws one item at a time, giving a verbal direction for the child to do the same thing. For example, the adult might say, "Draw a large square in the center of the paper, with a small circle inside the square. Next, make a smiley face in the top left hand corner of the paper." After several directions, remove the barrier and compare the two pictures, discussing how they are different or similar. Let the child take turns being the one to give directions to the adult.

Variations

- Use lined paper, and give directions to copy sequences to encourage memory skills (for example, "Let's draw circles to make this pattern: red, blue, green, red, blue, green").
- While shapes and colors are easier to describe, this game is also fun when you make it more creative. For example, give directions for drawing the family pet, but add silly directions, like making a green tongue, or a dog wearing mittens.
- Draw while lying on your belly, or at a vertical surface to strengthen upper body skills.

■ 21 MY LISTENING GAME

Primary learning focus

- Auditory perception.

Materials needed

- Child-friendly books, stories, or songs.

Description

Select a word that is included multiple times in a particular story or song, and then read or sing to the child, instructing her to listen for that word. Each time the child hears the targeted word, she must perform a designated action, such as clapping hands, acting like an animal, or jumping up and down. You can make the action relevant to the story or song (for example, if the story is about dinosaurs and the target word is dinosaur, the child must stomp her feet like a dinosaur).

Variations

- Some children may find it easier to listen if they close their eyes.

- Experiment with speeding up or slowing down while you read the story.

- Have the child hide under a blanket and jump out every time the target word is heard.

- For older children who can read, substitute listening for words that start with a targeted sound, or listening for words that fall into a particular category, like foods or animals.

22 COLOR ON COMMAND

Primary learning focus

- Auditory perception.

Materials needed

- Paper and markers or crayons.

Description

Draw a row of simple pictures, for example flowers, beach balls, Easter eggs, or a string of Christmas lights. Vary the number of items in the row according to how well the child can count and demonstrate one-to-one correspondence. Next, provide directions that require the child to process information, for example, "Color the first ball red and the sixth ball yellow."

Variations

- Do this with a partner, and have each partner take turns giving directions.

- Do this while lying on the belly, or at a vertical surface so that one hand has to hold the paper while the other hand colors.

23 DO YOU HEAR WHAT I HEAR?

Primary learning focus

- Auditory perception.

Materials needed

- Anything that makes a noise.
- Blindfold.

Description

Blindfold the child, and then activate common environmental sounds to see if the child can guess what you are doing (for example, turn on water, use a stapler, open the refrigerator door, pull down a window shade, tear a piece of paper, etc.)

Variations

- Turn on a fan or low volume music to create background noise, which increases the listening challenge.
- Make the sound more than once so the child has to count how many times the sound occurred as well as identifying what caused the sound.
- Create a sequence of different sounds for the child to guess.

24 COPY THE SOUND

Primary learning focus

- Auditory perception, motor planning, visual-motor integration, perception.
- Tends to be an energizing activity.

Materials needed

- Various noisemakers (commercial or homemade rhythm sticks, shakers, drums, etc.).

Description

Have the child sit facing away from you while you make a series of sounds using the instruments. See if the child can copy your sounds. Practice with loud/soft volume, and vary the speed from slow to fast.

Variations

- Have the child sit on a T-stool or yoga ball while doing this activity.
- Create some background noise to compete with the sounds to copy.
- Try doing this behind a closed door.

■ 25 MATCH THAT SOUND

Primary learning focus

- Auditory, fine motor strength and dexterity.

Materials needed

- A collection of same-sized containers (for example, paper lunch bags, empty film canisters, or opaque pill bottles).
- Assorted materials to place inside containers (for example, rice, beans, cheerios, paper clips, marbles, etc.).

Description

Create two sets of sound-makers, trying to use the same amount of fillers so that they sound exactly alike. Give the child one set, and stand across the room with the other. Choose one of the containers, shake it, and see if the child can find the one that sounds the same. Ask if he can guess what is inside (then open up and peek).

Variations

- Create background noise (for example music or a fan) to increase the listening challenge.
- Have two adults stand away from each other, shaking different containers, and ask the child "Who is shaking the … (marbles, rice)?"
- Have the child identify two different sound-makers, then copy sound sequences by holding one sound-maker in each hand and shaking according to a pattern.

OTHER IDEAS FOR SUPPORTING SENSORY SKILLS DEVELOPMENT

- Sitting in beanbags or rocking chairs for calming.
- Gentle roughhousing.

- Sit or lie on a blanket while two adults hold each end and provide a swing.

- Create a quiet area for self-calming, such as a table covered with a blanket and pillows on the floor.

- Use playground equipment for vestibular input (for example, swings and slides).

- Perform yoga poses.

- Use scented markers or dough.

- Use fidget toys (see Appendix B for ideas).

- Using weighted blankets, vests, or pencils for calming (see Appendix B for directions on how to make these items).

- Towel dry and apply scented lotion after a bath.

- Play in a sand box or at a water table.

- Play with Silly String.

- Use a vibrating toothbrush, toys, or pens.

- Wear tight fitting clothing such as leotards or neoprene shorts for calming.

- Blow whistles, flutes, pinwheels.

- Play games involving different head motions (like somersaults or cartwheels).

- Ride in elevators or on escalators.

- Guess different tastes or smells while blindfolded.

- Make a nature collage using different textured natural materials.

- Be thoughtful about choosing clothes for the child to wear to school. Avoid dressing in a way that might cause distractions (hair falling in the eyes, loose jewelry or tassels that create light touch sensations, ill-fitting shoes, pants that are too loose and tend to fall down, etc.).

REFERENCE GUIDE FOR SELECTION OF ACTIVITIES

Use this guide to identify which activities might be especially helpful for a particular child. Identify one or more areas of weakness for the child, then scroll down each column to select appropriate activities.

P = Primary focus of activity

S = Secondary focus of activity

A = Adaptations possible to address this skill

? = Typically addresses this skill, but each child reacts differently

Page	Activity	Gross motor strength	Body awareness	Motor planning	Balance	Bilateral integration	Fine motor strength	Dexterity	Eye-hand coordination	Attention/ tracking	Perception	Visual-motor integration	Calming	Energizing	Tactile	Auditory
27	Wheelbarrow walk	P	P	P	S	P			A				?			A
28	Angels in the snow	S	P	P		P					S				S	
28	Magic carpet	P	S	P	P	P			S		A		?			
29	Balance beam	S	P	P	P	A			A	S						
30	Making statues	P	P	S	P	S					A		?			
31	T-stool games	S	P	P	P	P		A	S	A						
31	Obstacle course	P	P	P	P	S		A	A	S	S	A		?		
32	Log roll	S	S	P		P	A							?		
33	Make-a-kite	P	S	P	S	P	S			S	S			?		
34	Belly time	P	P	P	A	S		A	A	A	A	A	?	?		
35	The supermarket game	P	P	P	P	S				S	A		?			A
35	Balloon twister	P	P	P	P	P			P	P				?		
36	Egg races	A	P	P	P	A			P	P				?		
37	Monkey toes	P	P	P	P	P			S		S			?		S
38	Crab-walk soccer	P	S	P	P	S			S	S				?		

Page	Activity	Gross motor strength	Body awareness	Motor planning	Balance	Bilateral integration	Fine motor strength	Dexterity	Eye-hand coordination	Attention/ tracking	Perception	Visual-motor integration	Calming	Energizing	Tactile	Auditory
38	Yoga balls	P	S	P	P	A	A	A	A	A	A	S	?		A	A
39	The popcorn game	P	S	P	P	P			S	S	A			?		
40	Zoom tube	P	P	P	S	P			S	S						
40	Scooping cups	P	P	P	P	S			S	S	A					
41	The dress-up race	P	P	P	S	P	P	P	S					?		A
42	Shadow maker	P	P	P	S	P		A	A				?			
43	Charades	S	P	P	S	P		S			S					
43	Rhythm sticks		S	P	P	P			P	A	S					A
44	I went to the gym…	P	P	P		P		A	A		S		?			S
50	Rainbow writing	A	A	P		A		P	S	S	P	P	?		A	S
51	Beat the clock		S	P		P	P	P	P	S		A				
52	Suncatchers			S		S	P	P	P	S	S				S	
53	Paper snowballs		S	P		A	P	P	P	S				?	S	
54	Windmakers	A	A	S		A	P	P	P	P						A
54	Go fishing	S	S	P	A	A			P	S	A					A

Page	Activity	Gross Motor					Fine Motor				Visual			Sensory			
		Gross motor strength	Body awareness	Motor planning	Balance	Bilateral integration	Fine motor strength	Dexterity	Eye-hand coordination	Attention/tracking	Perception	Visual-motor integration		Calming	Energizing	Tactile	Auditory
55	The marshmallow factory			P		P	P	P	P		P	P		?			
56	Secret envelopes	A	A	A	A	P	P	P	P	S						A	
57	Tap the ball	P	S	P		P			P	S	P						
57	Bubble blaster			P			P		P	P	A	A			?	A	
58	Putty games			P		S	P	P	S			A		?		S	
59	The turkey baster game		S	P		A	P	S	P	S				?			A
59	The muncher man		A	A		S	P	S	P	S				?			A
60	Grabber games			P		A	P	P	P	S	A	A		?			
61	Air traffic controller	S	S	P		P	P	P	P	S	S						
61	Bottle bowling	P	S	P	S	S	P		P	S	A				?		
62	Bubble wrap	A	S	A	A	P	P	P	P	S	A	A		?		A	
63	Rubber band ball			P		P	P	P	P	S	A			?		S	A
64	Tissue art			P			P	P	P	S	S	S				S	
64	Cutting sandwiches		S	P		P	P	P	P	P						S	
65	Haunted house	P		P	A	A	P	P	P	S	S	S					

Page	Activity	Gross motor strength	Body awareness	Motor planning	Balance	Bilateral integration	Fine motor strength	Dexterity	Eye-hand coordination	Attention/tracking	Perception	Visual-motor integration	Calming	Energizing	Tactile	Auditory
		Gross Motor					Fine Motor			Visual			Sensory			
66	Push-ins	A	A	P	A	A	P	P	P	A			?		A	
67	Button snake		S	P	A	P	P	P	P	P	A		?		S	
67	Homemade ring toss	A	A	P	A			S	P	S	S					
68	Treat boxes		S	P		P	P	P	P		P	P				
76	Gel bags						S	S	P	P	S	P	?		S	
76	Pompom magnets	A	A	S	A	A	P	P	P	P	P	P			S	
77	Marble roller	S	S	P		P			P	P	S	P				A
78	My color book			S		S		P	P	S	P					
79	Paddle ball	A	A	P	A	A			P	P						
79	Hide and seek for the eyes						A	A	A	P	P					A
80	Flashlight tag						A		P	P	P	P				A
81	Toothpick tunnel					P			P	P	P					
81	Puff ball	A	A	P					A	P	A		?			
82	The detective game					A		A	S	P	P					
83	Basic visual memory games								S	P	P	A				

Page	Activity	Gross motor strength	Body awareness	Motor planning	Balance	Bilateral integration	Fine motor strength	Dexterity	Eye-hand coordination	Attention/ tracking	Perception	Visual-motor integration	Calming	Energizing	Tactile	Auditory
84	Pattern memory games							S	P	P	P	P				A
85	Spoon relay		P	P	P	A			S	P	P		?			A
85	The dot map	A	S	P	A	P			S	P	P	A				A
86	Button box		S	P		P			P	P	A	A				A
87	Puzzling					P	P	P	P		P					
87	What's next?			A		A				P	P					
88	String art		S	P			S	P	P	P	P	P			S	
89	Homemade labyrinth game		S	P		P			P	P	P		?			
89	Homemade lacing cards		S	P		P	S	S	P	P	S		?		A	
90	Memory cards						A	P	S	P	P				A	
91	Making hidden pictures	A	S	P		P	S	A	P	P	P	P				
92	Finger pals		A		A			S	P	P	A					
92	Find-it bag		S	S	A			S	P	P	P	A	?			
93	The hole-in-one game		S	P		A			P	P						
103	Sensory search				A	A	S	P		S	A	A	?		P	A

Page	Activity	Gross Motor					Fine Motor			Visual			Sensory			
		Gross motor strength	Body awareness	Motor planning	Balance	Bilateral integration	Fine motor strength	Dexterity	Eye-hand coordination	Attention/tracking	Perception	Visual-motor integration	Calming	Energizing	Tactile	Auditory
103	Goop on a tray		A	A	A	A	A		S	S	A	P		?	P	
104	Spaghetti shapes	A	A	S	A	A		P	S	S	A	P			P	
105	Recipe for a squeeze		P						P		A		P		P	A
105	Edible chew necklace				A	P	P		P	S	A	S	?		S	A
106	Deep-sea diving for treasure		S					P			P				P	
107	Find that finger		P	A		S		A							P	
107	Don't shake the table games		P	P	A	A	A	P	P	P	S		P			
108	Pop goes the feeling	P	P	S	S	S	A	A				A	P			
109	Feel-it bag		S	S		A	A	P			P				P	
110	Egg timer errands	P	S	P	P	A		A	A				?	P		
111	Dizzy disks		S	P	P	A		A	P	S				P		A
111	My bouncing ball	P	S		P	A			S				?	?		P
112	Wall push-ups	P	P			S							P			
113	Dressing in the dark	P	P	P		P	S	P			A	A			S	A
114	Name that letter	A	S	A		A		A	A		A	P	?		P	A

Page	Activity	Gross motor strength	Body awareness	Motor planning	Balance	Bilateral integration	Fine motor strength	Dexterity	Eye-hand coordination	Attention/ tracking	Perception	Visual-motor integration	Calming	Energizing	Tactile	Auditory
		Gross Motor					Fine Motor			Visual			Sensory			
114	If I had a hammer	P	S	P		P	S	P	P	P	A	A	?			A
115	Blowing in the wind	P	A	A	A	A				P			?			
116	Name that tune		A	A	A	A			S							P
117	Mirror drawing	A	A	P		A	S	S	S		P	P				P
117	My listening game	A	A	A	A	A		A	A					?		P
118	Color on command	A	A	A		A	S	S	S							P
119	Do you hear what I hear?															P
119	Copy the sound	A	S	P	A	A	S		S		P	P		?		P
120	Match that sound			A		A		S								P

INSTRUCTIONS FOR HOMEMADE SUPPLIES

EQUIPMENT

T-STOOL

Materials

- 20cm (8") square of plywood, 2cm (¾") thick.

- 8cm (3") plywood square, 2cm (¾") thick.

- Wooden dowel, 2.5cm (1") diameter by 20cm (8") long.

- Eight 2.5cm (1") nails.

- One 3.8cm (1½") screw.

- One rubber crutch tip (available at pharmacies or medical supply stores).

Directions

- Sand the edges of the two wood squares to prevent splinters.

- Insert screw through the middle of the 8cm (3") plywood square into the dowel.

- Place the larger plywood square over the center of the smaller square and secure using nails.

- Place the rubber crutch tip over the bottom of the dowel.

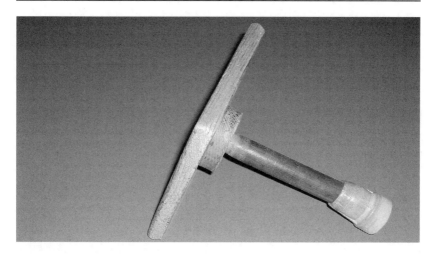

FIGURE B.1

ZOOM TUBE

Materials

- Empty toilet tissue roll.

- Contact paper.

- Markers, colored tape, stickers as desired.

- Two lengths of cord (slippery is better), each approximately 2.7m to 3m (9 to 10 feet) long.

Directions

- Tie loops onto both ends of the two cords to form handles.

- Cover the toilet tissue roll with contact paper, folding excess length over the ends of the tube (this makes the tube stronger and more slippery).

- Decorate the tube as desired.

- Insert one end of each cord into the tube.

- To use, two partners face each other, each holding one set of the handles with the zoom tube in the middle of the cords. Each partner steps back until the cords are taut. One partner brings her arms together, while the other partner brings her arms apart. This makes the tube "zoom" to the partner whose arms are together. By keeping the cords taut and carefully timing the opening and closing of arms, the tube will race back and forth between partners.

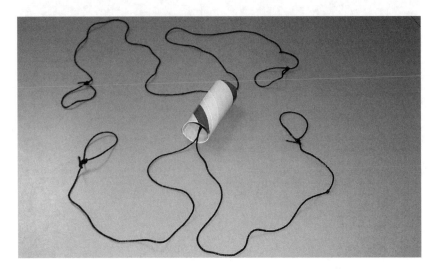

FIGURE B.2

SCOOPING CUPS

Materials

- Two large, clean, empty plastic bottles (such as those used to hold bleach, milk, or laundry detergent).

- Colored tape (plastic or duct tape).

- Lightweight object for throwing and catching (small beanbag, koosh ball, or crumpled wad of paper).

Directions

- Cut off the bottoms of both bottles.

- Cover the cut edges with tape to make sure they are smooth.

- To use, place a beanbag or other object inside one bottle to use for toss and catch games.

Figure B.3

WINDMAKERS

Materials

- Assorted, empty squeeze bottles (for example, ketchup or mustard squeeze bottles, infant nasal aspirator, or empty nasal spray bottle).

- Permanent markers for decorating bottles.

- Cotton balls, small pompoms, or small pieces of tissue paper.

Directions

- Remove any labels from the bottles, then clean and dry well.

- Use markers to make faces on the bottles, with the nozzle serving as the nose.

- To use, squeeze the bottle so that the cotton ball or tissue moves.

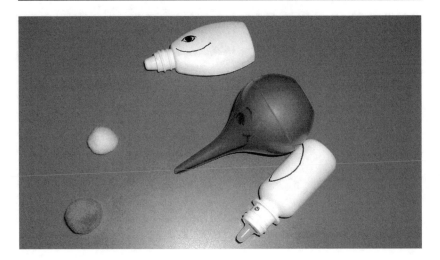

FIGURE B.4

SECRET ENVELOPES

Materials

- Assorted empty envelopes (used ones are fine).

- Wide-tip markers, or masking tape.

- Small prizes for the envelopes (stickers, secret messages, or a small edible treat).

- Scissors.

- Something to use as a tactile "launch pad" (for example, computer mouse pad, folded washcloth, sponge, or drink coaster).

Directions

- Place the prize inside the envelope at one end.

- Seal the envelope (use tape if recycling a used envelope).

- At the end of the envelope opposite to where the prize is hidden, create a path for the child to cut, using either the marker or tape (for more tactile input).

- Use the "launch pad" for the child to rest her hand on during cutting, teaching that the pinky side of the hand stays down towards the table, and the thumb side of the hand points to the ceiling.

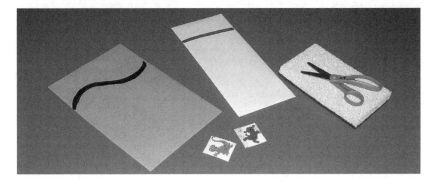

FIGURE B.5

TAP THE BALL

Materials

- Lightweight plastic ball with holes (for example, Wiffle ball).

- String.

- Wooden dowel or empty cardboard tube, approximately 45cm to 60cm (18" to 24") long.

- Colored tape or markers.

Directions

- Tie the string to the ball, and suspend from a tree branch or door still so that it is at the child's eye level.

- Use the tape or markers to create three lines around the dowel or tube, with one color forming a ring around the center, and two other colors forming rings approximately 15cm (6") from the ends of the dowel or tube.

- Holding the dowel at each end, the child faces the hanging ball and practices various tapping patterns while keeping the ball's movement steady and well controlled.

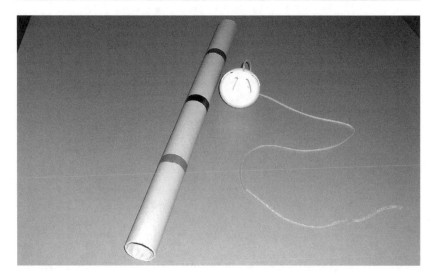

FIGURE B.6

MUNCHER MAN

Materials

- Tennis ball.

- Sharp razor knife.

- Permanent markers.

- Small objects to "feed" the muncher man.

Directions

- Carefully slice a 6cm to 8cm (2½" to 3") line along the seam that separates the fuzzy parts of the ball—this becomes the muncher's mouth.

- Use a red marker to color in lips around the cut, and other markers to add other facial features.

- The child holds the muncher man in her palm, positioned so that the thumb is at one end of the cut and the other fingers are at the other end of the cut. By squeezing at these points, the muncher man's mouth will open and close.

Figure B.7

BUTTON SNAKE

Materials

- Felt or fleece fabric cut into rectangles or ovals approximately 8cm (3") in size (these fabrics work best because they will not fray).

- Scissors.

- Buttons.

- Thread and needle.

Directions

- For the body pieces, sew a button onto one end of each piece, and cut a buttonhole at the other end.

- Make a head with only a buttonhole at one end, and a tail with only a button at one end.

- Use the pieces to practice buttoning and unbuttoning.

- Alternatively, use cardboard pieces, hole puncher, and brass paper fasteners (brads) to make a toy snake to play with.

FIGURE B.8

TREAT BOXES

Materials

- Empty cardboard boxes.

- Long, thick shoelaces, with different colors and textures.

- Something to punch holes in the cardboard boxes (screwdriver, awl, knitting needle).

- Small treats or stickers.

Directions

- Cut shoelaces in half, and then tie two different shoelace halves together. This will create a shoelace that has different colors and textures on each side.

- Punch two holes in the bottom of the box.

- Thread the two ends of the shoelace into the bottom of the box from the inside.

- Place the lid back on the box, and wrap the shoelace around the outside of the box.

- Teach the child to tie a bow around the box, using the two different colored laces to help the child to learn the steps of tying.

- If desired, find several boxes of different sizes that can nest together.

- If desired, use a treat or sticker to place in the box as a reward for good effort.

FIGURE B.9

GEL BAGS

Materials

- Large, freezer storage bag with zipper-style closure.
- Colored hair gel.
- Lighter fluid (optional).
- Duct tape.
- Small bead or button.
- Glitter or sequins.

Directions

- Try to find a clear bag without any writing on it. For some brands of bag, the white writing is easily removed using lighter fluid and a paper towel.

- Squirt enough gel into the bag to create a thickness of approximately 0.6cm (¼") when the bag is placed on its side.

- Place the bead or button, plus some glitter or sequins, into the bag.

- Close the zipper, squeezing out as much air as possible.

- Seal the closure with duct tape to prevent spilling.

FIGURE B.10

MARBLE ROLLER

Materials

- Marble.

- Bottle cap just large enough to cover the marble, or half of the smallest sized plastic Easter egg.

- Small wiggle eyes or other decorations for the marble roller.

- Lightweight plastic tray, empty box top, or cookie sheet.

- Paper and markers.

Directions

- Using paper and markers, make a variety of worksheets to use for rolling the marble (this could be mazes, simple dot-to-dots, letters of the alphabet or numbers). Place one paper on the tray.

- Decorate the bottle cap or Easter egg half as desired to make it into a creature or robot.

- Place the cap over the marble, then place it on one of the papers on the tray.

- Instruct the child to use both hands to hold the tray and maneuver the roller along a desired route.

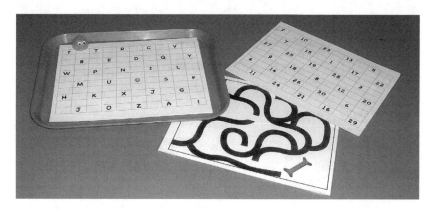

FIGURE B.11

PADDLE BALL

Materials

- Bendable coat hanger.
- Nylon hosiery.
- Foam for padding.
- Duct tape.
- Balloons.

Directions

- Bend the coat hanger to form an oval shape with a handle.

- Cut off one leg of hosiery (or use a knee-high) and slip it over the metal loop, securing it with tape around the handle.

- Use tape to secure the hosiery to the handle.

- Wrap the handle with foam to make a soft, padded handle, and cover with more duct tape.

- Blow up one or more balloons and use with the paddle.

FIGURE B.12

LABYRINTH GAME

Materials

- Rectangular piece of cardboard, cardboard tray, or empty cardboard box lid.

- Mazes (make your own, or refer to Appendix C for advice as to where to find free printable mazes online).

- Drinking straws.

- Scissors.

- Hot glue gun or tacky glue.

- Marble.

Directions

- Draw or print mazes large enough that the paths will fit the marble.

- Cut straw lengths to fit the lines of the maze and glue in place.

- Allow to dry.

- Place the maze inside a tray or empty box lid (if using a cardboard rectangle, add straw pieces to the sides of the rectangle to prevent the marble from rolling off the edges).

- To use, the child holds the labyrinth with both hands and attempts to maneuver the marble through the maze.

Figure B.13

FIND-IT BAG

Materials

- Large, sturdy freezer storage bag with zipper-style closure (can also use an empty 2 liter soda bottle or other type of clear plastic tube).

- Lighter fluid (optional).

- Identical pairs of assorted small objects (elastic bands, beads, buttons, avoiding sharp points or edges that might puncture the bag).

- Filler, such as sand, uncooked rice, poly beads (found in craft stores), or colored seed bead.

- Duct tape.

Directions

- Separate each pair of objects, placing one of each inside the bag or bottle, and reserving the other in a separate container.

- If using a zipper bag, try to find a clear bag without any writing on it. For some brands of bag, the white writing is easily removed using lighter fluid and a paper towel.

- Place enough filler to fill the bag or bottle to about three-quarters full.

- Close and seal the container with duct tape (if using a bag, try to remove some of the excess air so the filler and objects are easy to move around in the bag).

- To use, show the child one of the reserved objects, and see how quickly the child can find it in the bag or bottle.

FIGURE B.14

HOLE-IN-ONE

Materials

- One or more empty cardboard tubes (from toilet tissue or paper towels).

- Length(s) of string approximately 45cm (18").

- Ping-pong ball.

- Hot glue gun.

- Colored tape.

Directions

- To make a single hole-in-one, glue one end of the string to the ping-pong ball, and tie or glue the other end of the string to the cardboard tube.

- To make a multiple hole-in-one, place additional cardboard tubes adjacent to the single hole-in-one, tape together, and use different colors of tape around the edges of each tube.

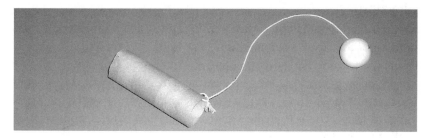

FIGURE B.15

NON-EDIBLE RECIPES
KNEADING DOUGH WITH FLOUR
Ingredients
1 cup flour
½ cup salt
1 tsp cream of tartar
1 cup water
1 tbsp cooking oil
Food coloring

Directions
Place all ingredients except food coloring in a saucepan and cook over medium heat until the mixture begins to pull away from the sides of the pan to form a ball. Remove from heat and cool, then add food coloring and knead until smooth. Store in an airtight container or plastic zipper bag. This makes a very soft dough similar to Play-doh.

FLOURLESS KNEADING DOUGH

Ingredients

1 cup baking soda
½ cup cornstarch
⅔ cup lukewarm water
Food coloring (optional)
Clear nail polish or shellac (optional)

Directions

Mix the baking soda and cornstarch in a pot, then add water and stir until smooth. Cook over medium heat until it comes to a boil and assumes a texture like mashed potatoes. Pour onto a board to cool, and knead, adding food coloring if desired. This dough will stay pliable for several weeks in an airtight container, but hardens quickly when exposed to air. Use it to make sculptures, leave to harden, and paint or shellac when dry.

SCENTED KNEADING DOUGH

Ingredients

85g (3 oz) sugar-free gelatin, any flavor or color
2 cups flour
1 cup salt
4 tbsps cream of tartar
2 cups boiling water
2 tbsps cooking oil

Directions

Mix all of the dry ingredients in a pot, and then add the boiling water and cooking oil. Stir over medium heat until the mixture forms a ball. Allow to cool. Store in an airtight container and refrigerate when not in use.

HOMEMADE FINGERPAINTS

Ingredients

1 cup flour
2 tsp salt

3 cups cold water
3 cups boiling water
Food coloring

Directions

Mix the flour and salt together in a pot. Add the cold water, stirring until smooth. Add the boiling water, and cook over medium heat, bringing to a boil and stirring continuously until clear. Then add the desired food coloring and cool before use.

PUFFY PAINT

Ingredients

1 cup flour
1 cup salt
1 cup water
Tempera paint to add color

Directions

Mix the first three ingredients, and then add tempera paint as desired to color the paint. Put the paint into squeeze bottles for painting. This paint puffs up and hardens when dry, creating a fun texture.

HOMEMADE SILLY PUTTY (WARNING — DO NOT INGEST!)

Ingredients

1 cup white Elmer's glue (do not substitute another brand)
1 cup liquid starch
Small amount of food coloring, if desired

Directions

Put glue and food coloring (if desired) into a plastic container. Add starch, a little at a time, stirring constantly until the mixture holds together like putty. Keep checking the texture and add very small amounts of starch until the putty feels smooth and rubbery. This is great putty for stretching, bouncing, transferring comic pictures, or burying small objects to find. Store in an airtight container. Can be refrigerated if the child enjoys a cold temperature.

SOAP CRAYONS

Ingredients
1¾ cups powdered Ivory Snow soap flakes
¼ cup water
Food coloring

Directions
Mix soap flakes and water together. Add food coloring and pour into ice trays or other molds. Allow to harden, and then remove from the molds. These are especially fun to play with in the bathtub!

EDIBLE RECIPES

IRISH POTATOES

Ingredients
½ cup warm mashed potatoes (no milk, salt or butter)
907g (2 lbs) confectioner's sugar (approximate)
½ tsp vanilla extract
Cinnamon

Directions
Add the vanilla to the warm mashed potatoes, and then add confectioner's sugar, a little at a time until the mixture forms a dough. Form into small balls and roll in cinnamon. These should be kept in the refrigerator and eaten the same day.

NUTTY PUTTY

Ingredients
1 cup peanut butter
½ cup honey
2 cups confectioner's sugar
Chocolate chips, raisins, etc. for decorating (optional)

Directions

Mix the peanut butter, honey, and confectioner's sugar, kneading until the mixture forms a dough. This can be shaped into small shapes or figures and decorated as desired. Store in the refrigerator in an airtight container. CAUTION: not appropriate for children with peanut allergies.

CANDY CLAY

Ingredients

½ cup light corn syrup
113g (¼ lb) softened margarine or butter (not melted)
½ tsp salt
1 tsp vanilla extract
4 cups confectioner's sugar

Directions

Blend the corn syrup and softened butter in a bowl. Add salt, vanilla extract, and confectioner's sugar. Knead with the hands until smooth. Store in an airtight container in the refrigerator.

BUGS IN DIRT

This recipe is a great motivator for children who dislike mixing the textures of food.

Ingredients (individual portion)

Snack size container of chocolate pudding
2 chocolate sandwich cookies
Gummi worms or bugs

Directions

Scrape the frosting off the cookies, and then let the child crush them with her hands into a bowl. In a plastic drinking cup or other tall container, alternate layers of pudding, cookie crumbs (the dirt!) and worms.

ANTS ON A LOG

This is another good recipe for mixing food textures.

Ingredients
Celery sticks
Peanut butter
Raisins

Directions
Spread peanut butter on the celery sticks, and then line up raisins (ants) on the log. CAUTION: not appropriate for the child who has a peanut allergy, but you can substitute cream cheese.

SLURPEES

Sucking food through a straw is calming and organizing for many children. The following are just some suggestions for foods appropriate for slurping. Experiment with crazy straws and thinner cocktail straws, which tend to require a stronger suck.

Slurpee foods
Milkshakes
Fruit smoothies
Apple sauce
Pudding, thinned with milk
Yogurt drinks

TOOTHPICK TREATS

This makes a fun snack, and encourages children to taste different textures and to practice their fine motor skills at the same time. Cut an assortment of foods into small cubes (think raw fruits and vegetables, cheese, chunks of meat, salad croutons, or goldfish crackers). Provide the child with a toothpick, and let her stab the food with the toothpick to eat!

BREAD PAINT

Ingredients
1 tbsp milk
4 drops food coloring
Light colored bread

Directions
Mix the milk and food coloring in a small bowl (make as many colors as desired). Use a small paintbrush to paint designs or secret messages on the bread, and then use the bread to make toast, sandwiches, or French toast (the colors will remain true even if the bread is cooked or toasted).

HEALTHY ALERTING SNACKS

In general, foods that are cold, crunchy, or have a strong, sour taste are alerting for the child who under-registers sensory information. The following are suggestions for snacks to help these children:

- crunchy raw fruits and vegetables
- crunchy granola or granola bars
- pretzels
- rice cakes
- air popped popcorn
- whole grain dry cereal
- sugar-free sour candy or gum
- fruit juice or sugar-free koolaid, frozen in ice cube trays
- graham crackers spread with yogurt and put in the freezer.

HEALTHY CALMING SNACKS

Foods that require a lot of chewing, along with those that are sticky and need "mouth work" to swallow tend to be more calming for children with high energy levels. Examples include:

- nut butters (be cautious about potential allergies)

- cream cheese or other spreadable cheeses

- raisins or other dehydrated fruits

- fruit leathers without added sugar

- nitrate-free meat jerky

- dense breads (such as bagels).

FAVORITE FIDGETS

Many children enjoy having a small toy or tactile object to keep in their hands when they need to be quiet or to concentrate in school. Occupational therapists refer to these as "fidget toys." The trick is to teach the child that a fidget is something to use quietly (not to play with), and is a tool to help them to maintain a calm body. If a fidget becomes distracting, it is taken away. Some children enjoy having a shoebox or other small container where they can keep a supply of several fidgets and choose one as needed. Others like to keep one in their pocket, or a few in a fanny-pack to carry around during the day. A few commercial fidgets have clips that can be attached to a belt loop or backpack strap so it is readily available. Use common sense when choosing fidgets, for example avoiding small objects that could cause a choking hazard if the child is prone to putting things in her mouth.

In my experience, teachers are very variable in their tolerance for children using fidgets at school. Some are happy to accommodate the child; others are concerned about the potential for distraction to the child as well as to her peers. Some of my favorite, quieter fidgets include:

- squeeze balls—these are readily available, or you can make your own using latex balloons and cornstarch. Use a funnel and chopstick to force cornstarch into a balloon until it is a little larger than a golf ball, tie it off, stuff it into a second balloon, and tie off again. This makes a fascinating texture to quietly squish

- a large nut and bolt to twist on and off

- worry beads (string a few onto a string or chenille pipe stem fastened into a circle)

- wrist coil key ring (with the metal key ring removed)

- a small bendable toy (like a Gumby doll or a bendable pencil)

- small koosh ball (some are made into key rings that can attach to a belt loop).

- small, smooth pebble for the pocket (if desired, use a permanent marker to write a secret reminder, like "Stay cool!")

- rubber band ball

- braided, knitted or crocheted necklace or bracelet using fancy yarns that have interesting textures.

WEIGHTED TOOLS

Children who have sensory processing differences often crave deep pressure and proprioceptive inputs. Using weighted garments or tools can be very calming and organizing to some children, and are often included as part of a therapy program. Commercial products are readily available, but unfortunately can be prohibitively expensive. The following sections provide directions for making some simple weighted tools at a much lower cost than purchasing commercially. If you choose to try these, remember that they should be used under supervision (especially if there is risk of the weighted filling leaking). Do not use items made with poly pellets or other small weighted materials if the child is prone to chewing on clothing or blankets. In the event a seam should break, the small pellets could cause a serious choking hazard. There is no absolute standard for how much weight to use, but my recommendation for home use would be to use approximately 5 percent of the child's body weight, unless directed otherwise by a professional. Weighted garments should never be worn for long periods of time, because the child acclimatizes to the sensation after about 20 minutes, making it no longer helpful. As a general rule, weights should be used for about 20 minutes, with at least a 20 minute "break" before they are used again.

LAP BLANKET

Materials

- Approximately 90cm (one yard) of flannel in a child-friendly pattern (or use a flannel pillowcase).

- Sewing machine with polyester thread.

- Approximately 1.4kg (3 lb) of poly pellets (these can be found in craft stores or online).

- Funnel.

Directions

- Fold the flannel in half, printed sides together, and sew the two long sides and one short side to make an open-ended rectangle (or use a purchased pillowcase).

- Turn the rectangle so the printed side is on the outside.

- Sew eight straight seams along the length of the rectangle, forming eight channels.

- Using the funnel, pour one and a half cups of poly beads into each channel.

- Sew the open seam at the end of the rectangle closed.

- Lay the rectangle flat, and using your hands, push the beads so that half are on each side of each channel.

- Sew a seam down the middle, forming two sets of eight channels with an equal distribution of poly beads in each channel.

- Repeat this process, until you have a rectangle divided into eight by eight channels.

- The lap blanket can be hand washed and air dried (do not use a washer or drier in case a seam fails and spills the poly pellets).

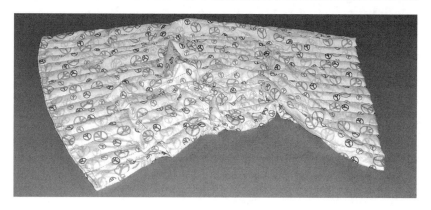

FIGURE B.16

VEST

Materials

- Child sized fisherman's vest with lots of pockets.

- Cloth for making beanbags.

- Sewing machine with polyester thread.

- Poly pellets.

Directions

- Use cloth to make beanbags approximately 9cm to 10cm (3½" to 4") in size, filling each beanbag with half a cup of poly pellets.

- Place finished beanbags in the pockets of the vest, making sure that weight is evenly distributed.

- Remove beanbags before washing the vest.

SENSORY SNAKE

Materials

- One men's extra-long white tube sock.

- Poly pellets.

- Fiberfill padding.

- Sewing machine.

- Large wiggle eyes.

- Hot glue gun.

Directions

- Fill the sock with alternating layers of fiberfill padding and poly pellets, using approximately 450g (1 lb) of the poly pellets.

- Sew the open end closed.

- Glue wiggle eyes onto the toe end of the sock.

- Use as a soft weight around the neck and shoulders, or as a lap weight.

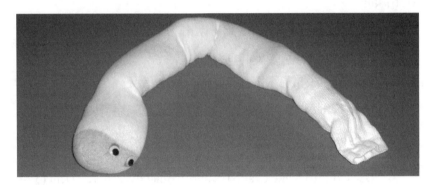

Figure B.17

WEIGHTED PENCIL

Materials

- Pencil.

- Metal nuts to fit the diameter of the pencil.

- Hot glue gun.

Directions

- Glue two or three nuts around the pencil shaft (above the area where the child will hold the pencil).

Appendix C

FURTHER RESOURCES

RECOMMENDED ORGANIZATIONS AND WEBSITES FOR INFORMATION AND GUIDANCE ABOUT CHILDREN WITH DISABILITIES

American Association on Intellectual and Developmental Disabilities
501 3rd Street NW, Suite 200
Washington, DC 20001, USA
Telephone: +1 (202) 387-1968
Website: www.aaidd.org

This organization promotes progressive policies, sound research, effective practices, and universal human rights for people with intellectual and developmental disabilities.

American Occupational Therapy Association
4720 Montgomery Lane, PO Box 31220
Bethesda, MD 20824–1220, USA
Telephone: +1 (301) 652-2682
Website: www.aota.org

This is the professional membership organization of occupational therapists in the United States. It offers consumer information including how to find an occupational therapist.

American Physical Therapy Association
1111 North Fairfax Street
Alexandria, VA 22314–1488, USA
Telephone: +1 (800) 999-2782
Website: www.apta.org

This is the professional membership organization of physical therapists in the United States, and offers a variety of consumer resources.

American Speech-Language Hearing Association
2200 Research Boulevard
Rockville, MD 20850–3289, USA

Telephone: +1 (800) 638-8255
Website: www.asha.org

This is the professional membership organization of speech therapists and audiologists in the United States. It has a section dedicated to providing information and resources for consumer audiences.

Association of University Centers on Disabilities
1100 Wayne Avenue, Suite 1000
Silver Springs, MD 20910, USA
Telephone: +1 (301) 588-8252
Website: www.aucd.org

This is the home organization for University Centers for Excellence in Developmental Disabilities, which are supported by federal funding and legislation in the United States. These centers serve as the bridge between the academic arena, and public policy and services. They focus on the training of advanced level practitioners, dissemination of state-of-the-art knowledge, and in some cases, direct service for individuals with developmental disabilities.

Autism Independent UK
199–203 Blandford Avenue
Kettering, Northants NN1 9AT, UK
Telephone: +44 (0) 1536 523274
Website: www.autismuk.com

This useful website offers many information resources for parents and professionals, including an extensive listing of links to worldwide resources pertaining to autism.

Autism Society of America
4340 East-West Highway, Suite 350
Bethesda, MD 20814, USA
Telephone: +1 (800) 328-8476
Website: www.autism-society.org

This organization provides information and referral services for children with autism.

Center for Disability Information and Referral: Kids Corner
Website: www.iidc.indiana.edu/cedir/kidsweb

This is a wonderful website for children to access information about what it is like to have a disability. It includes links to games, books, celebrities who have disabilities, movies and television shows featuring persons with disabilities, and more!

CHADD National
> 8181 Professional Place, Suite 150
> Landover, MD 20785, USA
> Telephone: +1 (800) 233-4050
> Website: www.chadd.org

> This organization sponsors continuing education programs for parents and professionals, as well as parent support groups for children with ADHD.

Children's Defense Fund
> 25 E. Street NW
> Washington, DC 20001, USA
> Telephone: +1 (800) 233-1200
> Website: www.childrensdefense.org

> This agency provides information about United States federal legislation pertaining to child health, welfare, and education. It publishes a consumer guide describing parent rights under the Individuals with Disabilities Education Act.

College of Optometrists in Vision Development
> 215 W. Garfield Road, Suite 200
> Aurora, OH 44202
> Telephone: +1 (330) 995-0718 or +1 (888) 268-3770
> Website: www.covd.org

> This website offers extensive resource information on the role of vision in autism, ADHD, and learning disabilities, as well as a directory of qualified developmental optometrists.

Council for Exceptional Children
> 2900 Crystal Drive, Suite 1000
> Arlington, VA 22202–3557, USA
> Telephone: +1 (888) 232-7733
> Website: www.cec.sped.org

> This is an association for parents and professionals with an interest in children with developmental differences. It provides literature reviews, referrals, and computer searches on topics related to developmental disabilities.

Educational Resources Information Center (ERIC)
> Website: www.eric.ed.gov

> Sponsored by the United States Department of Education, this website produces the world's premiere database of journal and non-journal education literature, with many full-text articles offered to consumers at no charge.

Future Horizons
> 721 West Abram Street
> Arlington, TX 76013, USA
> Telephone: +1 (800) 489-0727
> Website: www.fhautism.com

This organization offers extensive listings of publications and continuing education opportunities pertaining to autism. It also offers links to other autism-related websites.

Learning Disabilities Association of America
> 4156 Library Road
> Pittsburgh, PA 15234–1349, USA
> Telephone: +1 (412) 341-1515
> Website: www.ldaamerica.org

This organization disseminates information, provides advocacy, and seeks to improve education opportunities for individuals with learning disabilities.

National Autistic Society
> 393 City Road
> London EC1V 1NG, UK
> Telephone: +44 (0)20 7833 2299
> Website: www.nas.org.uk

This organization offers resources and services for children with autism and their families residing in the United Kingdom.

National Center for Learning Disabilities
> 381 Park Avenue South, Suite 1401
> New York, NY 10016, USA
> Telephone: +1 (888) 575-7373
> Website: www.ncld.org

This agency provides public awareness of learning disabilities by publishing a magazine for parents and professionals, and by providing site-based information and referral services.

National Dissemination Center for Children with Disabilities (NICHCY)
> PO Box 1492
> Washington, DC 20013, USA
> Telephone: +1 (800) 695-0285
> Website: www.nichcy.org

This serves as the central source of information on children with disabilities in the United States. It includes easy to read information on the federal regulations governing early intervention and special education services, and provides state resource sheets for accessing these resources.

Optometric Extension Program
    1921 E. Carnegie Avenue, Suite 3–L
    Santa Ana, CA 92705–5510
    Telephone: +1 (949) 250-8070
    Website: www.oepf.org

    This website offers extensive articles and resources on the topic of vision
    and disabilities.

Optometrists Network
    58 Mohonk Road
    High Falls, NY 12440
    Website: www.optometrists.org

    This website offers a directory of participating optometrists, as well as
    useful articles, and links to other websites relating to learning disabilities.
    It also contains child-friendly pages that discuss vision difficulties, games
    and screening tests for older children, and a link to anecdotal reports
    from parents whose children have shown success following vision
    therapy.

Pacer Center, Inc.
    8161 Normandale Boulevard
    Bloomington, MN 55437, USA
    Telephone: +1 (800) 537-2237
    Website: www.pacer.org

    This is a parent information and training center for families of children
    and youth with all types of disabilities. It offers publications, workshops,
    and other resources including a national bullying prevention center.

Sensory Processing Disorder Foundation
    5420 S. Quebec Street, Suite 135
    Greenwood Village, CO 80111, USA
    Telephone: +1 (303) 794-1182
    Website: www.sinetwork.org

    This website offers a wealth of information pertaining to sensory
    processing disorder, including research, treatment options, and tips and
    strategies for children and families.

Sensory Smarts
    Website: www.sensorysmarts.com

    This website provides great information about sensory processing,
    including how to find an occupational therapist, suggestions for sensory
    diet activities, practical suggestions for common problems at home
    and school, and where to find specialty toys and products addressing
    sensory needs.

Special Needs UK

Website: www.specialneedsuk.org

This website offers comprehensive information about schools and parent support groups for children of all ages within the United Kingdom.

United Kingdom Government

Website: www.gov.uk/children-with-special-educational-needs/overview

This government sponsored link outlines the process for obtaining assessment and special education services for children with special needs in the United Kingdom.

United States Department of Education

Website: http://idea.ed.gov

This governmental link provides a description of the federal Individuals with Disabilities Education Act, which provides for early intervention, special education, and related services to children ages 0 through 21 residing in the United States.

Zero to Three: National Center for Infants, Toddlers, and Families

1255 23rd Street

Washington, DC 20037, USA

Telephone: +1 (202) 638-1144

Website: www.zerotothree.org

This is a non-profit, multidisciplinary organization that serves to inform, educate, and support adults who influence the lives of infants and toddlers.

OTHER RECOMMENDED ACTIVITY GUIDES

Angermeier, P., Krzyanowski, J. and Moir, K.K. (2009) *Learning in Motion: 101+ Sensory Activities for the Classroom,* 2nd edition. Arlington, TX: Future Horizons.

Arwine, B. (2011) *Starting Sensory Therapy: Fun Activities for the Home and Classroom.* Arlington, TX: Future Horizons.

Beckerleg, T. (2008) *Fun with Messy Play: Ideas and Activities for Children with Special Needs.* London: Jessica Kingsley Publishers.

Biel, L. and Peske, N. (2005) *Raising a Sensory Smart Child: The Definitive Handbook for Helping Your Child with Sensory Integration Issues.* New York: Penguin Books.

Brack, J.C. (2009) *Learn To Move, Moving Up! Sensorimotor Elementary-School Activity Themes.* Shawnee Mission, KS: Autism Asperger Publishing Co.

Brack, J.C. (2004) *Learn To Move, Move To Learn.* Shawnee Mission, KS: Autism Asperger Publishing Co.

Brady, L.J., Gonzalez, A.X., Zawadzki, A. and Presley, C. (2011) *Speak, Move, Play and Learn With Children on the Autism Spectrum.* London: Jessica Kingsley Publishers.

Bruni, M. (2006) *Fine Motor Skills for Children with Down Syndrome: A Guide for Parents and Professionals.* Bethesda, MD: Woodbine House.

Delaney, T. (2009) *101 Games and Activities for Children with Autism, Asperger's, and Sensory Processing Disorder.* New York: McGraw-Hill.

Drew, S. and Atter, E. (2008) *Can't Play Won't Play: Simply Sizzling Ideas to get the Ball Rolling for Children with Dyspraxia.* London: Jessica Kingsley Publishers.

Griffin, S. and Sandler, D. (2009) *Motivate to Communicate! 300 Games and Activities for Your Child with Autism.* London: Jessica Kingsley Publishers.

Haldy, M. and Haack, L. (1999) *Making It Easy: Sensorimotor Activities at Home and School.* San Antonio, TX: Psychological Corporation.

Hickman, L. and Hutchins, R.E. (2010) *Eyegames: Easy and Fun Visual Exercises: An OT and Optometrist Offer Activities to Enhance Vision,* 2nd edition. Arlington, TX: Sensory World.

Jacobs, D.S. (2012) *Everyday Activities to Help Your Child With Autism: Simple Exercises to Boost Functional Skills, Sensory Processing and Coordination.* London: Jessica Kingsley Publishers.

Jereb, D. and Jereb, K. (2010) *Move About Activity Cards.* Arlington, TX: Sensory World.

Koscinski, C. (2012) *The Pocket Occupational Therapist for Families of Children With Special Needs.* London: Jessica Kingsley Publishers.

Kranowitz, C. (2006) *The Out-Of-Sync Child Has Fun: Activities For Kids With Sensory Disorder,* revised edn. New York: Perigee Trade.

Kurtz, L.A. (2008) *Understanding Motor Skills in Children with Dyspraxia, ADHD, Autism, and Other Learning Disabilities.* London: Jessica Kingsley Publishers.

Kurtz, L.A. (2006) *Visual Perception Problems in Children with ADHD, Autism, and Other Learning Disabilities.* London: Jessica Kingsley Publishers.

Moor, J. (2008) *Playing, Laughing and Learning with Children on the Autism Spectrum: A Practical Resource of Play Ideas for Parents and Carers,* 2nd edition. London: Jessica Kingsley Publishers.

Sher, B. (2009) *Early Intervention Games: Fun, Joyful Ways to Develop Social and Motor Skills in Children With Autism Or Sensory Processing Disorders.* Hoboken, NJ: Jossey-Bass.

Smith, B.A. (2011) *From Rattles to Writing: A Parent's Guide to Hand Skills.* Framingham, MA: Therapro, Inc.

Smith, B.A. (1998) *The Recycling Occupational Therapist: Hundreds of Simple Therapy Materials You Can Make.* Tucson, AZ:Therapy Skill Builders.

Tilley, K. (2011) *Active Imagination Activity Book: 50 Sensorimotor Activities for Children to Improve Focus, Attention, Strength, and Coordination.* Arlington, TX: Sensory World.

Winders, P.C. (1997) *Gross Motor Skills in Children With Down Syndrome: A Guide For Parents and Professionals.* Bethesda, MD: Woodbine House.

Zysk, V. and Notbohm, E. (2010) *1001 Great Ideas for Teaching and Raising Children with Autism or Asperger's,* 2nd edition. New York: McGraw-Hill.

FREE ONLINE RESOURCES FOR SENSORIMOTOR LEARNING

Activity Village (www.activityvillage.co.uk)

This website is an extensive resource offering free learning games and activities for children.

All Kids Network (www.allkidsnetwork.com)

This website offers a wealth of craft ideas, worksheets, games, and puzzles.

Artists Helping Children (www.artistshelpingchildren.org)

This site includes an extensive list of homemade toys and crafts for children of all ages, with very clear, easy to follow directions and many free printables.

Blue Bonnet Village (www.bluebonnetvillage.com/recipes.htm)

This website has a great list of simple recipes for homemade clay, craft dough (including several that are edible), and paints.

Brain Connection (www.brainconnection.positscience.com)

This website has a section offering online brainteasers and memory games, generally more difficult and geared towards teenager or young adult audiences.

Childhood101 (www.childhood101.com/playopedia)

This website offers a comprehensive reference network of unique play ideas organized by different categories of play.

Dance Mat Typing (www.bbc.co.uk/schools/typing/flash/stage1.shtml)

Free, on-line, typing games and activities for all levels of keyboarding skill.

DLTK (www.dltk-kids.com)

This popular website has links to a wide range of craft ideas, worksheets, and printables. It features especially helpful ideas for holidays and educational themes.

Eye Can Learn (www.eyecanlearn.com)

This website offers free activities and exercises designed to improve visual tracking scanning skills, eye teaming, and visual perception skills.

Free Preschool Crafts (www.freepreschoolcrafts.com)

This website includes a wonderful collection of craft ideas using inexpensive and recycled materials.

Free Typing Games (www.freetypinggame.net)

This website offers free, theme-based games for learning keyboarding skills.

Handwriting Worksheets (www.handwritingworksheets.com)

This website offers custom-made handwriting practice sheets.

OT Mom Learning Activities (www.ot-mom-learning-activities.com)

Developed by an occupational therapist, this website suggests a wide range of activities to support sensorimotor learning with clear photographs of children participating in each activity.

PapaJan (www.activitypad.com)

This website offers many printable games and activities suitable for preschoolers, as well as a variety of online games to help develop visual attention and perception.

Printable Mazes (www.printablemazes.net)

This website offers free downloadable mazes, mostly suitable for older children.

School Sparks (www.schoolsparks.com)

This website offers a wide variety of free worksheets for developing school readiness skills, with particular emphasis on improving auditory perceptual skills, visual discrimination, and fine motor skills.

Small School OT (https://sites.google.com/site/smallschoolot)

Developed by an occupational therapist, this website offers extensive activity resources and internet links for parents, teachers, and students.

Therapy Fun Zone (www.therapyfunzone.com)

This website features activities recommended by occupational therapists and physical therapists, including free printables (activities, cutting templates, pencil fun templates, paper folding templates). Therapy toys and materials are also sold at this site.

Therapy Street (www.therapystreetforkids.com)

> A website offering activities and printables, as well as fun recipes for putty, fingerpaints, and various tactile games.

Your Therapy Source (www.yourtherapysource.com/freestuff.html)

> This website offers a wide range of activities suitable for therapy or special education needs.

BOOKS THAT INTRODUCE YOUNG CHILDREN TO CONCEPTS RELATED TO DISABILITIES AND SENSORY PROCESSING DISORDER

Band, E.B. and Hecht, E. (2001) *Autism Through a Sister's Eyes*. Arlington, TX: Future Horizons.

> (Asperger's and high-functioning autism, ages 8 and older)

Betancourt, J. (1995) *My Name is Brain Brian*. Danbury, CT: Scholastic Paperbacks.

> (Learning disabilities, ages 8 and older)

Birdseye, T. (1996) *Just Call Me Stupid*. New York: Puffin Books.

> (Dyslexia, ages 8 and older)

Edwards, B. and Armitage, D. (2012) *My Brother Sammy is Special*. New York: Sky Pony Press.

> (Autism, ages 5 and older)

Fenner, C. (1997) *Yolanda's Genius*. New York: Aladdin Publishers.

> (Learning disabilities, ages 8 and older)

Filing, V. (1997) *Be Good To Eddie Lee*. New York: Philomel Books.

> (Down syndrome, ages 4–10)

Gainer, C. (1998) *I'm Like You, You're Like Me: A Child's Book About Understanding and Celebrating Each Other*. Minneapolis, MN: Free Spirit Publishing Inc.

> (General disability, ages 5–9)

Harding, J. (2011) *Ellie Bean The Drama Queen: A Children's Book About Sensory Processing Disorder*. Arlington, TX: Sensory World.

> (Sensory processing disorder, ages 5–9)

Hoopman, K. (2012) *Inside Asperger's Looking Out*. London: Jessica Kingsley Publishers.

> (Asperger's, ages 5 and older)

Hoopman, K. (2008) *All Dogs Have ADHD*. London: Jessica Kingsley Publishers.

> (ADHD, ages 5 and older)

Hoopman, K. (2006) *All Cats Have Asperger Syndrome*. London: Jessica Kingsley Publishers.

(Asperger's, ages 5 and older)

Hoopman, K. (2001) *Of Mice and Aliens*. London: Jessica Kingsley Publishers.

(Asperger's, ages 6 and older)

Janover, C. (2000) *How Many Days Until Tomorrow?* Waldoboro, ME: Goose River Press.

(Dyslexia, ages 8 and older)

Kraus, J. (2004) *Cory Stories: A Kid's Book About Living With ADHD*. Washington, DC: Magination Press.

(ADHD, ages 5–10)

Lears, L. (1998) *Ian's Walk: A Story About Autism*. Morton Grove, Il: Albert Whitman & Company.

(Autism, ages 5 and older)

Lewis, B. (2007) *In Jesse's Shoes: Appreciating Kids With Special Needs*. Grand Rapids, MI: Bethany House Publishers.

(Sibling issues, ages 4–9)

Lowell, J. and Tuchel, T. (2005) *My Best Friend Will*. Shawnee Mission, KS: Autism Asperger Publishing Co.

(Autism, ages 5 and older)

Moss, D. (2006) *Shelley, the Hyperactive Turtle*. Bethesda, MD: Woodbine House.

(ADHD, ages 4–9)

Nadeau, K.G. and Dixon, E.B. (2004) *Learning To Slow Down and Pay Attention*, 3rd edition. Washington, DC: Magination Press.

(ADHD, ages 6 and older)

Ogaz, N. (2008) *Buster and the Amazing Daisy*. London: Jessica Kingsley Publishers.

(Asperger's, ages 10 and older)

Peralta, S. (2002) *All About My Brother: An Eight-Year-Old Sister's Introduction to Her Brother Who Has Autism*. Shawnee Mission, KS: Autism Asperger Publishing Co.

(Autism, ages 4 and older)

Polacco, P. (2012) *Thank You, Mr. Falker*. New York: Philomel.

(Learning disabilities, ages 5–8)

Renna, D.M. (2007) *Meghan's World: The Story of One Girl's Triumph Over Sensory Processing Disorder*. Center Moriches, NY: Indigo Impressions.

(Sensory processing disorder, ages 5 and older)

Robb, D.B. (2004) *The Alphabet War: A Story About Dyslexia.* Morton Grove, IL: Albert Whitman & Co.

(Dyslexia, ages 7–10)

Rothe-Fisch, M. (2009) *Sensitive Sam: Sam's Sensory Adventure Has a Happy Ending.* Arlington, TX: Future Horizons.

(Sensory processing disorder, ages 6 and older)

Schnurr, R.G. (1999) *Asperger's Huh? A Child's Perspective.* Ottowa, Ont.: Anisor Publishers.

(Asperger's, ages 6–12)

Shriver, M. (2001) *What's Wrong With Timmy?* New York: Little Brown Books for Young Readers.

(Mental retardation, ages 2–6)

Smith, M. (1997) *Pay Attention, Slosh!* Grove, IL: Albert Whitman & Company.

(ADHD, ages 8 and older)

Steiner, H. (2012) *This Is Gabriel, Making Sense of School: A Book About Sensory Processing Disorder*, 2nd edn. Arlington, TX: Sensory World.

(Sensory processing disorder, ages 7 and older)

Thompson, M. (1992) *My Brother, Matthew.* Rockville, MD: Woodbine House.

(Mental retardation, ages 4–10)

Tourville, A.D. (2010) *My Friend Has Autism.* Mankato, MN: Picture Window Books.

(Autism, ages 5 and older)

Tourville, A.D. (2010) *My Friend Has ADHD.* Mankato, MN: Picture Window Books.

(ADHD, ages 5 and older)

Tourville, A.D. (2010) *My Friend Has Down Syndrome.* Mankato, MN: Picture Window Books.

(Down syndrome, ages 5 and older)

Tourville, A.D. (2010) *My Friend Has Dyslexia.* Mankato, MN: Picture Window Books.

(Dyslexia, ages 5 and older)

Veenendall, J. (2009) *Why Does Izzy Cover Her Ears? Dealing With Sensory Overload.* Shawnee Mission, KS: Autism Asperger Publishing Co.

(Sensory processing disorder, ages 6 and older)

Veenendall, J. (2008) *Arnie and His School Tools: Simple Sensory Solutions That Build Success.* Shawnee Mission, KS: Autism Asperger Publishing Co.

(Sensory processing disorder, ages 6 and older)

Welton, J. (2008) *Adam's Alternative Sports Day: An Asperger Story.* London: Jessica Kingsley Publishers.

(Asperger's, ages 8 and older)

Wilson, L.F. (2009) *Squirmy Wormy: How I Learned To Help Myself.* Arlington, TX: Sensory World.

(Autism and sensory processing disorder, ages 6 and older)

Wine, A. (2005) *What It Is To Be Me! An Asperger Kid Book.* Fairdale, KY: Fairdale Publishing.

(Asperger's, ages 4 and older)

Zimmett, D. (2001) *Eddie Enough!* Rockville, MD: Woodbine House.

(ADHD, ages 4 and older)

GLOSSARY

Accommodation: the ability to use the eye muscles to focus as objects move closer or farther away from the eyes.

Ambyopia: the loss of visual acuity due to disuse of vision as opposed to acuity impacted by a refractive error or eye disease. Also referred to as "lazy eye."

Auditory processing disorder: difficulty understanding and responding to sounds or language.

Bilateral integration: The neurologic process of organizing sensations from both sides of the body to allow smooth, coordinated, and reciprocal movement between the two body sides.

Binocular vision: the ability of the visual system to convert the images from each eye into a single image for the brain to interpret.

Body awareness: (see proprioception).

Depth perception: using the visual feedback from both eyes to judge the distance of an object.

Developmental milestones: skills that most children can be expected to achieve at a predictable age, for example, taking a first step at 11 to 13 months of age.

Developmental optometrist: an eye care professional with advanced training vision problems related to childhood development and learning.

Discriminative tactile sensations: perception of tactile input leading to an awareness of the size, shape, temperature or texture of an object, or of body sensations like hunger or thirst.

Distal: pertaining to parts of the body that are far away from the midline or the trunk.

Double-jointedness: having an increased range of motion in a joint compared to others.

Dynamic balance: maintaining balance while the body is in motion, for example when walking across a balance beam or climbing stairs.

Dyslexia: a specific learning disability characterized by difficulty learning to read fluently and with good comprehension despite normal intelligence.

Dyspraxia: limited ability to plan and carry out unfamiliar motor activities with skill. Also referred to as poor motor planning.

Education Act of 1996: this is the legislation that governs access to a broad and balanced National Curriculum for students with physical or learning disabilities residing in the United Kingdom.

Endurance: the ability to sustain physical effort over time.

Extraocular muscles: also called the extrinsic eye muscles—the six muscles that surround and control the movement of each eye.

Feedforward: sensory information that helps to predict what is needed to perform an action successfully; for example, when catching a ball, vision informs the speed and size of the ball to be caught, and proprioception informs whether the hands are positioned correctly.

Fine motor: referring to the smaller muscles of the hands, mouth, and eyes that are involved in precision movements.

Gross motor: referring to the larger, weight bearing muscles that control posture, balance, and large movements such as those involved in walking, running, or climbing stairs.

Hyperresponsive: unusually alert to a sensory experience.

Hypertonia: (see muscle tone).

Hyporesponsive: unaware of a sensory experience that others would typically notice.

Hypotonia: (see muscle tone).

Individuals with Disabilities Education Act (1996): Along with the Individuals with Disabilities Improvement Act of 2004, this United States legislation provides for a free and appropriate education for all eligible students with disabilities ages birth through 21.

In-hand manipulation: moving objects within the hand using only the small muscles of the hand.

Manual dexterity: skill and ease with which one can use the hands to perform rapid, automatic fine motor movements.

Motor planning: (see praxis).

Muscle tone: The degree of tension present in muscles when at rest or when passively moved, which may range from low to high; children with low tone (hypotonia) typically have poor posture and increased joint mobility, while children with high tone may have stiff movements and limited flexibility.

Perceptual reasoning: the ability to understand and find relationships between visually presented, non-verbal stimuli, such as pictures or objects; a set of skills related to overall intelligence that are typically a good indicator of problem solving and organizational skills.

Postural stability: the ability to control the center of mass in relation to the base of support in order to feel steady, to move with control, and to prevent falling.

Praxis: Also called motor planning—the ability to plan, organize, sequence, time, and execute unfamiliar motor activities in a skillful manner.

Proprioception: the unconscious sensation of body position and movement that stems from sensory receptors in the joints, muscles, and tendons.

Proximal: pertaining to parts of the body that are close to the midline or the trunk.

Protective tactile sensations: tactile sensory experiences that alert the person to potential danger and trigger a reflexive need to move away from that danger.

Radial: pertaining to the side of the hand closest to the thumb.

Section 504 of the Rehabilitation Act of 1973: This is a United States civil rights law that prevents discrimination to citizens with disabilities when they access publicly funded resources. In certain situations, children with disabilities or health-related concerns may be eligible for accommodations to their public school program under this act.

Sensory reception: the process that occurs when an organ of reception (such as the eyes or the ears) is stimulated by an event (such as a visual image or a sound), so that that information can be transmitted to the brain for interpretation.

Sensory integration: the brain's way of organizing sensory inputs to allow for an adaptive response.

Sensory integration disorder: problems with filtering or interpreting sensory inputs needed for learning or behavioral self-regulation—sometimes referred to as sensory processing disorder.

Sensory modulation: The ability to appropriately filter sensory input in order to maintain an appropriate level of alertness and behavioral self-regulation.

Sensory perception: the brain's interpretation of sensory experiences.

Sensory processing disorder: (see sensory integration disorder).

Spatial awareness: an awareness of one's body in space, and the relationship of one's body to other objects in space.

Special Education Needs (SEN): this is the umbrella term used in the United Kingdom to describe those aspects of public school education focusing on students with physical or learning disabilities.

Static balance: maintaining balance while the body is still, for example standing on one foot without falling.

Strabismus: poor alignment of the eyes.

Strength: the amount of force produced during a muscle contraction.

Tactile defensiveness: problems with perception of certain tactile experiences often leading to strong emotional reactions, hyperactivity, or other behavioral difficulties.

Ulnar: pertaining to the side of the hand closest to the pinky finger.

Vestibular: pertaining to the sensory system, located within the inner ear, that provides information about gravity, body movement within space, and head position. This sense plays an important role in balance, motor planning, and coordinated eye movements.

Visual acuity: the ability to see clearly. Problems seeing things that are far away is called nearsightedness, and problems seeing things up close is called farsightedness.

Visual attention: the ability to apply conscious effort to focus and persist with viewing a visual stimulus.

Visual closure: the ability to recognize pictures or forms that are incomplete.

Visual form constancy: an understanding that visual stimuli can look different, yet mean the same thing, such as a word presented in different fonts or styles of writing.

Visual discrimination: the ability to use vision to recognize the basic attributes of an object, such as size, shape or color.

Visual efficiency disorders: problems with eye muscle control that make it hard to maintain visual focus or to visually track a moving target.

Visual figure-ground discrimination: the ability to separate foreground from background visual stimuli in order to focus on the most important details.

Visual memory: The ability to recall visually presented information.

Visual-motor integration: the ability to coordinate visual information with fine or gross motor skills to produce a well-executed response to an environmental demand requiring motion.

Visual perception: an assortment of information processing skills that allow a person to understand what is seen.

Visual sequential memory: the ability to recall a series of visual stimuli in the correct order.

Visual-spatial perception: the ability to recognize the orientation and position of an object relative to other objects or to oneself.

Working memory: immediate recall of information that has been recently presented.

LIST OF ACTIVITIES